LOVE

LOVE

An Unromantic Discussion

Mary Evans

polity

First published in 2003 by Polity Press in association with Blackwell Publishers Ltd, a Blackwell Publishing Campany.

Editorial office:
Polity Press
65 Bridge Street
Cambridge CB2 1UR, UK

Marketing and production:
Blackwell Publishers Ltd
108 Cowley Road
Oxford OX4 1JF, UK

Published in the USA by
Blackwell Publishers Inc.
350 Main Street
Malden, MA 02148, USA

A catalogue record for this book is available from the British Library.

Library of Congress Cataloging-in-Publication Data
Evans, Mary, 1947–
    Love, an unromantic discussion / Mary Evans.
        p. cm.
    Includes bibliographical references and index.
    ISBN 0-7456-2072-8 (alk. paper) — ISBN 0-7456-2073-6 (pbk. : alk. paper)
    1. Love. I. Title.
    HQ801 .E93   2002   2002003173

Typeset in 11 on 13pt Sabon
by Graphicraft Limited, Hong Kong
Printed in Great Britain by MPS Books, Bodmin, Cornwall

This book is printed on acid-free paper.

For David, Tom and Jamie

Contents

Acknowledgements   viii

1 What is this Thing Called Love?   1
2 Going Back   25
3 The Language of Love   56
4 The Rules of Love   79
5 The Limits of Love   104
6 The Future of Love   124

Notes   144
Bibliography   155
Index   162

Acknowledgements

I have very much enjoyed writing this book. By that I mean that I have enjoyed exploring the various issues involved in the text, as well as the process of writing about them. In that process a number of people have given me considerable help and assistance. To Carole Phillips my thanks are due for her patient typing of the manuscript; through this she enabled me to write by hand and continue a practice apparently disapproved of in some universities. The staff of the Templeman Library at the University of Kent have been endlessly helpful and have made that library a great pleasure to use. The Beaney Institute in Canterbury has also generously ordered and borrowed books for me and demonstrated the appeal of a genuinely public library. To all these people, and to Anne Phillips, Sally Harris and many other colleagues at the University of Kent and elsewhere I am extremely grateful for their consistent general support as well as interest in this project.

1

What is this Thing Called Love?

There is nothing that the human heart more irresistibly
seeks than an object to which to attach itself.

William Godwin

The pursuit of love has engaged human energy for centuries.
That comment implicitly assumes, as a great deal of writing
about love also does, that the emotion which we describe in
the West as 'love' is about personal, emotional relationships.
We no longer also assume that all love is about heterosexual
love (or between people of the same age, race and religion)
but our association of love is with an individual relationship which also involves a sexual relationship.[1] Although
we use the word love to indicate our feelings for objects,
situations and ideas, most people, in thinking of love, would
probably associate the word with love for another, chosen,
person. Despite the fact that for many people the greatest
loves of their lives are their children (or their parents) it is
love for unrelated others which dominates our present thinking, and expectations, about the subject. Indeed, some of
the more famous declarations of affection (such as that of
the biblical Ruth to her mother-in-law, 'Whither thou goest,
I will go') are often subsumed into romantic discourse.

The way in which we construct love, which is the subject of this book, has long been the concern of writers and artists. The highs and lows of love have been recorded on miles of canvas and forests of paper. From this tradition has emerged the consensus that romantic love is both deeply desirable and extremely difficult to achieve, let alone maintain. Thus we grow up, and are socialized into, a set of expectations about love which both endorse the aspiration of romantic love and are sceptical about its achievement. We hope that through love we will end the emotional loneliness of adult life but have to confront, like Levin in Tolstoy's *Anna Karenina*, the stark truth that the loved other is not only unable to offer perfectly realized intimacy, but is also another person. We associate being in love, and the state of bliss of love, with the love sonnets of John Donne ('For love all love of other sights controls'[2]) but seldom read the more sombre, later, poems of Donne in which he professes his recognition of the limits of earthly loves and passions.

Donne's acknowledgement of the disappointments, as well as the joys, of love was first published in the seventeenth century. Since that time 'love' has never been absent from the agenda of writers, artists and moralists in the West. Love matters, not just to us as individuals, but to society and the social world in general because it is the language, the understanding and the behaviour through which we organize our sexuality and our personal lives. It is because of this that love has recently acquired a place amongst the concerns of sociologists and social historians: 'love', it would seem, is becoming more problematic and is giving rise to confusions and contradictions which have a destabilizing effect on the social world. It is this question which is the concern of this book: what does 'love' mean to us at the beginning of the twenty-first century and is it an emotion, and an expectation, which we should abandon or continue to pursue? Dare we entertain the idea of a world without love and could another vocabulary, in which words such as care, commitment and desire were more often used, actually make us happier? Would we, could

2

we, live more fulfilled and contented lives without the emotional state which we describe as 'love'?

The possibility that individual happiness, organized around 'love', is becoming more difficult to achieve in the West (despite generally improved living standards, access to contraception and the economic emancipation of women) has begun to attract considerable attention, not least because the problems of 'love' have been linked to what is described as the 'breakdown' of the family. That breakdown has been much exaggerated, and often viewed – as is much else in the contemporary West – in an ahistorical way, so that there is little understanding of long-term instabilities in the family (resulting, for example, from death or migration). But social pundits concerned with what they see as the increasing fragmentation of social life are quick to identify 'selfish' attitudes to personal life and love. Against these voices (amongst which can be identified that of the journalist Melanie Phillips) are sociologists such as Anthony Giddens and Ulrich Beck who have argued that personal life has become not more chaotic than ever, but more democratic.[3] In the view of Giddens, 'intimacy' (by which he means primarily, although not exclusively, relations between women and men) is being transformed in ways which offer the possibility of a 'pure' relationship. (A 'pure' relationship is one founded upon the autonomy of both parties and their ability to relate to each other as separate, functionally and emotionally competent adults). For Giddens, love is no longer tied to sexuality and those 'pure' relationships which he values are entered into for 'their own sake'.[4] Like the majority of writers on love, he shares much of the Western language of love, in which love between adults is essentially a matter of individualized attraction, although one which can now exist within a new moral framework. The cornerstone of that framework, the new 'democracy' of intimacy, is that the relationship need only continue, in Giddens's words, 'in so far as it is thought by both parties to deliver enough satisfaction for each individual to stay within it'.

Cynics (both feminist and otherwise) might argue that this is exactly how many men have always viewed relationships with women, as relationships that need only continue as long as they are satisfactory to men. The difference – according to Giddens – is that now the ending of relationships need not take place within a rhetoric of blame or the assumption of the economic abandonment of women. It is tempting to read Giddens's account of the democratization of intimacy as an optimistic male rationalization (and legitimation) of a new order of Western gender relations made possible by the economic emancipation of women. But for Giddens the new order benefits women as much as men, a view challenged by, amongst others, Wendy Langford. Her case, to be discussed later, emphasizes many of the persisting inequalities of gender which Giddens tends to minimize. But the argument here is less with the politics of gender in Giddens than with his account of the politics of the social world. There is a consensus amongst sociologists that there has been a shift in late modernity towards a new rhetoric and a new set of expectations about some aspects of gender relations. It would be extraordinary if the 'language of love' did not change as other aspects of the social world change. Nevertheless, the question of how, and why, that language changes remains problematic. To assume, as Giddens does, that the 'new' organization of love in the twenty-first century will create more democratic societies and civil cultures is extraordinarily optimistic. To suppose that changes in the private world will bring about corresponding changes in the public world is to ignore the strength of those public institutions and structures which are far from democratic.

When demonstrators against the war in Vietnam famously confronted the National Guard of the United States by placing flowers in the barrels of guns, they created a vivid image about power in the West. Those demonstrators contributed to the ending of the war in Vietnam; but whilst political opinion was changed, the structural order of political power was not. Since the 1960s individuals in

4

the West have known greater personal freedoms, albeit in terms which have been identified as 'repressive tolerance'. As those critics of mainstream Western culture have argued, this greater personal sexual freedom has neither changed the absolute sum of human happiness or unhappiness (although the forms may have shifted) nor made significant inroads on the structural distribution and organization of economic and political order. On the contrary, and a theme for discussion here, it is possible to argue that greater sexual 'freedom' has increased personal dissatisfaction and had a destabilizing effect on everyday life. The expectations of romance and sexual pleasure within intimacy which are the subject matter of the various dream factories of the West endlessly threaten the fragile possibilities of human happiness. Perhaps most significantly, we have become less able to recognize the limits and boundaries of love: the 'democratization of intimacy' is thus more about the democratization of the miseries and the disappointments of love than about an increase in its many rich pleasures.

Thus the discussion of love has come to the attention of social pundits largely because it has become clear that love, and most specifically heterosexual love, has disruptive social consequences. As a consequence of being 'in love', or falling 'out of love', individuals change partners, move house and leave behind jobs, homes and children. Economists in the United States have remarked that divorce and separation are good for business, in that people who leave home generally have to engage in setting up another home. In setting up this new home (and often beginning to live – as increasing numbers of people do – alone) individuals have to buy all those household goods they left behind or did not manage to take with them. The slogan published in Britain in the Second World War ('Careless Talk Costs Lives') was never more true than in the contemporary politics of love and romance. The fateful admission of love, or its lack, literally changes lives and creates consequences not just for the individuals concerned, but for those others involved in the relationship. Those 'others' are notably children, who may grow up, particularly in Britain and the United States, as the results of vanished 'loves'. The familiar mantra of 'Mummy/Daddy and I no longer love each other, but will always love you' has become part of the lives of many children, who experience in real life the vagaries of love portrayed in television soap operas. It would no doubt startle many viewers if a character in the British soap opera *EastEnders* admitted that even though 'love' had disappeared from a relationship, they would nevertheless stay in it for the sake of the children, social respectability or religious principles. Love, or its absence, as an acceptable motive for individual action has become part of the expectations of our culture. We take it as a form of socially sanctioned and accepted individual entitlement that the presence or absence of love legitimates the establishment or the ending of personal relationships; the moral force of the idea that parents should stay together for the 'sake of the children' has largely disappeared from our culture.

Thus, as many of us experience the increasingly diverse and general controls on our lives associated with complex industrial societies, love, and our love relationships, may appear to be becoming less controlled as moral codes and taboos change or fragment. As women and men of the twenty-first century we are allowed to go out and look for love, on what is supposed to be the newly level playing field of relations between women and men. There is no longer the expectation that men will express feelings of love in order to persuade women into sexual relationships or that women will exchange sexuality for love. That such exchanges still occur, and are still part of many people's assumptions, does not invalidate the fact that the expectation is no longer held as the normal or single discourse of love. It is permissible for sexual desire to be openly expressed by both women and men and for a separation to be made between sexual desire and romantic and emotional attachment. A popular culture exists throughout the

West in which fleeting sexual encounters are regarded, if not as necessarily normal or desirable, then certainly as commonplace. This has allowed moral judgements about sexual behaviour to move to other aspects of sexuality, such as those of deceit or care with contraception. Establishing a morality for the 'new' sexuality remains a contentious issue: but in that debate 'love' still plays a considerable part, in that in the absence of other forms of social control it remains an informal, but generally recognized, sanction.[5]

Love, in our present use of the term, can only be seen as a changing code. To look for 'real love' in the history of love (or the literature about it) will lead us, assuredly, to find many different meanings and expressions of the word. The fixed point in this context will be the question of the social implications of love. Sociologists (and historians and literary critics) have come to recognize that love matters in social, just as much as in individual, terms. As Stevi Jackson has pointed out, contemporary sociologists fall 'in love' and in part, no doubt, because of this have started to re-engage with a subject that initially attracted previous generations.[6] Max Weber, Georg Simmel, Talcott Parsons and Jürgen Habermas have all noted the connection between romantic love and modernization.[7] Indeed, nobody brought up and educated in European bourgeois culture could fail to notice that a generalized discourse of romantic love, as we now know it, first made its significant appearance at the end of the eighteenth century when women, just as much as men, become active participants in the discourse of romance. Just as ideas about human freedom and autonomy challenged the practice and ideology of slavery, so the language of romantic love began to allow women a greater, legitimate part in the negotiation of marriage. The language of emancipated individualized love contained similar ideas to the debate about slavery: ideas about freedom, liberty, ownership and personal choice.[8] The expectation of mutual attraction began in which male and female partners had to make themselves lovable to the other party.

This expectation, which is now part of the gender relations of all Western societies, began to take certain recognizable forms in Europe in the late eighteenth century. These forms differed over time and in different contexts, but have increasingly come to form the cocktail of explicit sexual desire and shared secular interests which is the basis of contemporary, heterosexual, Western love. This is not to say that romantic love has only been invented in the past 200 years: the history of love includes Abelard and Héloïse, Romeo and Juliet as well as those Renaissance nuns described by Judith Brown as being 'passionately in love'.[9] But these loves existed as much outside marriage as within, and what became distinctive about constructions of love from the beginning of the nineteenth century was their identification with marriage: an identification which marginalized other 'loves' and created the expectations of marriage which are currently being renegotiated. A contest over the meaning of marriage was not an invention of the nineteenth century, but what was a significant departure was the expectation that romantic love was an essential part in both the construction and the continuation of marriage.

Unfortunately for many people this contest – and discussion – remains unresolved. The history of how 'love' has changed in the past 200 years is the subject of the next chapter, but in order to illustrate the dramatic difference that can exist between individuals from the same culture and society about love we need look no further than the case of the marriage of Prince Charles and Diana Spencer. This unhappy relationship dramatized the different expectations and aspirations that can exist about love, and the disastrous consequences for individuals if they do not share at least a measure of common understanding about the relationship between love and marriage. As spectators of this marriage we could all observe the havoc that these different expectations caused. We know that when asked, before the marriage, if he was 'in love', Prince Charles could only bring himself to admit to a doubtful yes, and the qualification 'whatever love means'. The tape has been frequently re-run to show either the honesty of Prince Charles, or his deceitfulness. On the one hand, he was a man who was genuinely confused about encoded messages in the discourses of late capitalism or on the other he was a two-timing deceiver who knew perfectly well his real affections were with a woman other than his fiancée. The constrained engagement interview essentially talked away the kind of single-minded passion which many individuals aspire to in love: the most positive characteristic of Lady Diana Spencer was, to her fiancé, that 'she was very energetic' and the most important question about their marriage was that 'lots of other people are involved'. 'Very energetic' could be taken as a coded reference to sexual enthusiasm and energy, or it could be a reference to the kind of energy associated with children and young animals. As a description of a loved one, and a singled-out loved one, it is not particularly flattering. On the other hand, what we now know about the circumstances in which Prince Charles went into this marriage (and his comment at the time that a lot of other people were involved in it) may lead us to suppose that the comment on Lady Diana's energy was a reflection on his lack of it.[10] A much older man confronting a young bride was faced, and hardly for the first time in recorded history, with the prospect of needs (both sexual and otherwise) greater than he could meet.

As episode succeeded unhappy episode in the sad saga of the Charles and Diana marriage, the global public saw a tired (both individually and generally) version of patriarchal, dynastic marriage confronted by a set of modern expectations about emotional life. Inevitably, critics, commentators, friends and relations lined up on either side of this contest, but there was little attempt to acknowledge the strengths, and horrors, of *both* sides of this domestic drama. The two central characters were world-famous, rich and privileged, but in their different ways each represented the considerable difficulties of resolving the question of both defining the meaning of love and showing how to implement that meaning. To begin with their respective families: each extraordinarily materially secure yet riddled with dissent and rage. On the Spencer side Diana's grandmother had virtually disowned her daughter, Diana's mother, whilst amongst the Windsors the children, and specifically Prince Charles, had been sacrificed to a homophobic regime of separation and brutality.[11] The personal misery inflicted in childhood and adolescence on all British male heirs apparent since the time of Queen Victoria was duly inflicted upon Charles, and what emerged was a man of erratic temper inside the faultless tailoring of royalty.[12] Charles, it was taken for granted, had to marry, and he did so in a way which demonstrated both the respect and the contempt for marriage which has long been a part of aristocratic understanding. Marriage is important as a social contract, because it secures succession ('the procreation of children', as the Church of England marriage ceremony states). Marriage is much less important as a relationship of realized and fulfilled personal love. Signing up to the contract of marriage as outlined by the Church of England (the procreation of children first, safety from 'sin' second and the mutual help and understanding of husband and wife a somewhat belated third) demonstrated a commitment to an understanding of marriage which has long been abandoned by many couples. The seventeenth-century prayer book was written a century before the first general emergence of romantic love in marriage and what it defines is an explicit distinction between ideals of union (which are part of a religion) and secular aspirations about behaviour. Reading the words of the Anglican marriage ceremony in the twenty-first century confronts us with a statement about marriage which is at odds with romanticized expectations.[13]

The expectations of Lady Diana Spencer were clearly for a 'modern', romantic, marriage and when she died there was a considerable body of opinion which suggested that she had been cheated out of this. That view obscured the reality of the marriage for the groom and his family in which the imperatives of succession outweighed other considerations. Diana Spencer's attempt at modernizing the British Royal Family ended not least because her view of romance and marriage was in many ways as anachronistic as that of her husband. The extreme individualization of her expectations, the interpretation of marriage as an exclusively individual relationship and the need for personal reparation through marriage were all part of one interpretation of the contemporary culture of romance. Given that these ideas are shared by many people, it was inevitable that Diana Spencer received, after her death, an extremely sympathetic press. Whatever the comments of her detractors, there is no doubt that she was mourned (for whatever reason) by millions. There was a general awareness that there was a considerable degree of projection and displacement involved in the public display of mourning, but even given this qualification, and reservations about the actual degree of public mourning, there was an unparalleled sense of general loss. Within two years of her death, Diana had become one of the great icons of the twentieth century. She had also become, in the essays of Julie Burchill and Beatrix Campbell, a feminist icon, a woman almost literally sacrificed to the tribal interests of the Windsors and betrayed by her own family and her husband's.[14] Burchill and Campbell have little sympathy for the institution of monarchy (a sentiment which they share with an increasingly large part of the British population) but what shines through the accounts of Diana by both women is their horror at the emotional manipulation and deceit involved in the Diana and Charles courtship and marriage. Whatever they, or anyone else, may think about the behaviour of Charles and Diana after the marriage, the contract of the marriage, and its initiation, transparently involved the misuse of social power. However much Diana Spencer was a silly girl who envisaged marriage as a series of new clothes and romantic exchanges, it nevertheless remains the case that we expect, as a culture, that age and power carry with them the responsibility of protecting the young from their own vulnerability. The corruption of minors is recognized in our culture as both a moral and (in the context of institutions) a social offence; and this form of behaviour was not altogether far removed from that of the Royal Family towards Diana.

This argument – which would obviously be entirely unpalatable to those who found Diana's behaviour in the marriage unacceptable – should not obscure Diana's often erratic and narcissistic actions. As Elizabeth Wilson and Joan Smith have pointed out, Diana was not a saint and had a limited understanding of the world.[15] It is not difficult to make out the case that Diana was an emotionally unstable individual. But in judgements about the individuals concerned (Diana was warm and loving, Charles was cold and deceitful versus Diana was selfish and wilful, Charles was well-meaning and kind) we lose sight of two issues: first, that in their different ways both Charles and Diana represented the many pitfalls of late twentieth-century constructions of love; and second, that just as the Establishment raged and closed ranks against Diana so those very similar conservative factions voiced concern – in debates about sexuality – for responsible adults to protect the vulnerable young.

Thus in the debates in the British parliament about the age of homosexual consent much was made of the issue of the power relations implicit in sexuality. The debates again brought to the surface the complex, contradictory views of our culture about sexuality and moral responsibility: some were prepared to argue that sixteen-year-olds were perfectly able to make autonomous decisions about sexual relationships whilst others put a much higher age on this ability. The issue is, inevitably, entirely a grey area in which legislation can intervene only clumsily and imperfectly. Nevertheless, the point of the debates is that they recognize that decisions about sexuality and sexual partners involve ideas, ideologies and discourses about questions related to love, desire and romance. In debates about these issues (generally related to questions of the age of consent) one thread remains consistent: that there are differences in power between people who contract or enter into sexual relationships. The argument that there should be no age of consent, and that there should be no legally enforced restrictions on sexual activity and access, remains deeply unacceptable to most people. Even if there is a tacit recognition that young people can be 'mature' (very often a code word for seductive), there is equally a strong sense that this 'maturity' should not, in itself, allow sexual activity.[16]

It was in the context of these debates that Charles courted and married his young bride. The marriage was presented, not least by the two participants, as a meeting of age and youth, of innocence and experience. Diana, presumably by personal choice, attired herself for her wedding in a dress which both concealed her body and kept her husband at a distance. She chose as bridesmaids and pages very young children and constructed an image of herself which associated her entirely with innocence, and a form of innocence which visually marginalized her sexuality. Thus the wedding dress and the clothes of the attendants suggested both innocence and distance. The rigid construction of the wedding dress disallowed the human form, whilst its elaboration (and extensive train) suggested a state of separation – literally, a virgin island. Against his bride, Charles appeared as a rigid figure of authority. Rather than marry in morning dress he chose military uniform, a uniform designed for the commanders of a vanished British Empire, and resonant with the associations of military rule and conquest. To say that the participants chose to marry wearing something approaching fancy dress suggests that they knowingly participated in masquerade. The problem, it became clear as the world became a party to the marriage (and the public was just as much the notorious third person in the marriage as Camilla Parker-Bowles), was that this was not fancy dress, but dress which called up living, real fantasies and not departed ones. The bride saw herself as an object of romance, the bridegroom saw himself as the embodiment of a particular kind of tradition. The former validated, indeed demanded, individual romantic choice, whilst the latter demanded the relegation of the individual to the general and the abstract. The television cameras which tried so hard to avoid the ranks of the divorced and separated amongst the families of the chief protagonists could not entirely dispel the impression of the unhappy meeting of two very different ways of organizing and constructing personal relations.

The same public which watched the wedding of Charles and Diana was the public which consumed the millions of miles of print about the marriage and its dissolution. Two miserable people fought for control of the public and private agenda of the marriage. At the service of each party were different constituencies: Diana could command the services of the media whilst Charles could call upon the services of significant sections of the British Establishment. The media – and most particularly the Murdoch press – was endlessly anxious to absorb Diana into its own industry of romance, whilst the Crown was concerned to maintain ancient privileges and hierarchy. As the saga unravelled, it became clear that Diana had to rely on essentially individualistic strategies: she could appeal or speak or act as a person, but her ability to do so was entirely dependent on appearing as a commercially attractive and appealing person. Her access to institutionalized power was far less than that of Prince Charles, who probably realized the limitations of being a commodity, however apparently marketable. The essential and final tragedy of Diana was that of her belief in the power of romance to provide happiness and even security against the risks of being driven too fast by a drunken driver. It is all too easy to envisage the final conversations of Diana's life in which a rhetoric of love ('you'll be safe with me', or 'I'll always look after you') was more persuasive than mundane comments about the dangers of excessive driving speeds. In endorsing a masquerade of romance, Diana became an object of its potential for destruction.

There now exists an extensive literature about the masquerades of masculinity and femininity.[17] Both sexes, whether gay or straight, can be seen to be acting out these masquerades – of which one is romance and the romantic in various forms of public display. Part of our contemporary performance of gender is the performance of the lover or the loved, in appropriately gendered ways. Every time that Diana chose to lower her eyes and look demure and frightened, she 'performed' femininity. From the bows on her wedding dress onwards, she consciously participated, through dress and body language, in a late twentieth-century urban game. Her difference from her husband lay, in part, in his refusal to recognize that he too was performing a part. Prince Charles, like many people in the culture, identified himself with 'normality' and 'the ordinary' and saw nothing constructed about either his sense of self or his appearance. That all appearance, and behaviour, is to a certain extent dictated by our fantasies about ourselves is a recognition impossible for those who cling on to the belief in the fixed and stable self.

Thus in this unhappy pair lay two competing discourses about the late twentieth-century self: neither good nor bad, better or worse, but fatally different. Within these different discourses lay radically dissimilar ideas about love and romance, and with that an intense competition for command of the private space. Inevitably, Diana at first seems the more attractive partner: more personally fluent and more apparently accessible, she appears to embody current expectations about the terms on which we engage with others: terms of intimacy, accessibility and absence of a sense of social hierarchy. To touch people with AIDS and to kneel down to speak to children suggests democratic attitudes to others. The physical posture says equality and shared experience of the same planet. On the other hand, to shake hands with people whilst often keeping one hand inside the jacket (as Prince Charles is apt to do) suggests at the very least a limited wish to share physical intimacy. Indeed both Charles and his father show a

15

marked inclination when in public to keep their hands under strict control, as if their hands might all too easily stray to forbidden places and people. There is, in the body language of both father and son, little of that willingness to touch, and allow oneself to be touched, which so differentiated Diana. Amongst a family remarkable for the wish of its female members to shake hands with strangers only when wearing gloves, Diana's reckless physical availability was immediately a mark of differentiation.

This sharing of the bodily space, and easy physical intimacy, is part of a Western culture which now allows, and to a certain extent expects, a paradoxical openness about the body. On the one hand, the body is a matter of intense display but, on the other, public expectations have come to assume scrupulously observed boundaries between bodies. Thus in public places, whether or not the body is clothed, we regard it as a basic right to remain literally untouched by others. The ideal physical presence of the late twentieth century is thus one which fluently performs its chosen sexual role but does not intrude in the performances of others. It is in this context – of a space for the body that is both permissive and restrictive – that people perform the rituals of love and romance for themselves and observe the performance in others. In the bridal pair of July 1981 millions of television viewers throughout the world saw the meeting of two cultures about the body and sexuality. Diana was instantly recognizable as a person of the late twentieth century: apparently easy with her physical self, fluent in her movements and conversant with the meanings attached to the body in the contemporary West. That this was not entirely the case was not immediately known: but as it became known and as the 'facts' of Diana's anorexia and bulimia became publicly available, what remained was a sense of a person who – whatever her personal problems with her own body – nevertheless lived within a particular, modern code of the body. This code recognized the ironic and performative possibilities of dress; it was conversant with ideas about the juxtaposition of

16

different kinds of dress; and, above all else, it made apparent the recognition of the self-consciousness of dress and physical appearance. When Diana dressed up as an erstwhile teenager, or the Madonna-like mother, the public recognized an engagement with performance through dress.

Performing ourselves has become a known and acknowledged part of both theoretical and actual practice.[18] Part of that performance, as much as it involves dress, bodily behaviour and public demeanour, also involves performing certain key social rituals. This aspect of our social lives has been noted for some time by sociologists: Erving Goffmann and subsequently Harold Garfinkel showed how, through the performance of certain forms of behaviour, we can convince others about our social identity.[19] For Goffmann, this ability was described most vividly in the context of *Asylums*, in Garfinkel's case his most dramatic instance was that of the male individual who convinced others that 'he' was actually female.[20] Cross-gender impersonation – and cross-class impersonation – have a long history and literature in the West, and what both show is that it is possible by the demonstration of certain key social characteristics to convince others of our social identity.[21] This tradition – often forgotten in discussions such as those by Judith Butler – assume that performance rituals are a distinctive feature of the modern world. Like much else that is assumed to be a unique feature of the contemporary world, performance as part of social life is a long-standing part of social existence. Judith Butler has focused on the performance by men and women of differentiated gender identities, but there are many other performances – related to class and ethnicity – which are equally important. When we say of others that 'I was taken in by their appearance', we say, in effect, that what we saw was the external self, which apparently resonated and seemed to meet our particular needs and desires. Our language about appearance contains expressions such as 'looking the part' and 'dressed for success', both ideas which contain the idea of 'putting on' a social identity.

But it is important to emphasize that what is also involved here is a complex expectation: as much as we recognize that people can 'dress up to' certain identities, we also expect them to fulfil those identities.[22]

Just as we 'perform' particular roles and identities of women and men, so we perform the roles of lover and loved. Thus Diana deliberately and publicly played the part of the damsel saved, or at least found, by Prince Charming. When this fantasy could not be sustained within marriage, and lacking as it did a partner willing to accept and play out a ritual of romance, Diana, and the public, chose another role associated with Western expectations of love – that of the woman scorned and deceived by a faithless husband. In the fiction of Diana's step-grandmother, Barbara Cartland, the end of the novel is always (as is the case of much 'great' literature) the beginning of the marriage. As many cynics have said at many weddings, 'That's the easy bit.' This note of caution, widely made and widely acknowledged, is the explicit recognition that men and women are brought together in marriage through fantasies as much as more mundane considerations. The West, at this particular historical point, makes much of its condemnation of arranged marriages, regarding them as part of the general barbarism of non-Western cultures. At the same time, the West equally deplores the high rates of divorce and separation that are part of heterosexual relationships. In this there is an extraordinary absence of social imagination – or even the ability to make connections between transparently related situations. Put simply, the West (in the form of its produced and everyday culture) endorses and validates romance, and yet cannot recognize that the encouragement of this set of feelings places a terrible burden of expectation on its participants. To be 'romantic' has always been associated with turning away from reality. In relations between men and women our apparently overwhelming need for romance would sometimes suggest that the reality of these relations is too awful to be allowed.

18

Within the marriage celebrated between Charles and Diana we know that neither partner found either romance or lasting love. What each person confronted, after the honeymoon was over (or even on it, if the stories of the marriage are to be believed), was a person with whom they had, in the language of everyday speech 'little in common'. To many outsiders, what they had in common was actually considerable, given that both parties were vastly over-privileged in terms of material possessions and had lived lives in which their social experience was limited to a tiny fraction of the population. (The Windsors are often described as a 'dysfunctional' family, but given their ability to maintain their grasp on power and privilege this is hardly an accurate description of their social, if not their emotional, competence.) Indeed, in terms of similarities of class, race and culture, the two parties were hardly miles apart. But what they did not have 'in common' and what proved to be the undoing of the marriage was a shared enthusiasm for, and agreement about, the meaning of love and romance. Thus on public (indeed global) display was dissimilarity and disagreement about perhaps the most individually significant ideology of our times: the question of how we organize our personal and emotional relationships. As inhabitants of complex societies (or as inhabitants of any society) we live in a set of rules, expectations and norms. Many of us (although by no means all) are much more free from material constraint than we were in the nineteenth century, but at the same time we are endlessly constrained by the demands of the labour market.[23] We have become 'free' in certain aspects of our lives (in that we are generally free from starvation and widespread disease) but on the other hand contemporary normative structures assume levels of social and personal success that are often unrealizable. A culture of rising material aspirations has become the norm of Western societies and with this expectation has come a culture which assumes the entitlement to personal and emotional fulfilment. The 'pursuit of happiness' was enshrined in 1776 in the constitution of the United States, but it is only in the past century that the full implications of that concept, in secular societies which have abandoned the self-limiting idea of the ultimate love for, and moral authority of, a God, have become clear. As Gillian Rose has suggested in *Love's Work*, the self-reliance of modernity 'leaves us at the mercy of our own mercilessness; it keeps us infinitely sentimental about ourselves, but methodically ruthless towards others'.[24] As a comment on the Diana/Charles marriage, the words are particularly apt in that they accurately describe the brutal personal revelations about the other made by husband and wife. In the same broadcast, Diana Spencer sentimentalized herself as a 'Queen of Hearts' while she ruthlessly damned her ex-husband's personal qualities.

In the secular social worlds of technologically developed and sophisticated societies the appeal of ideologies of love and romance are deeply seductive. In them we think we can find an area of life which is ours and ours alone and through which we can validate other aspects of our existence. We were told, in the 1950s, that 'love and marriage go together like a horse and carriage' and that the ideal woman was one who is 'so nice to come home to'. Even as these ideas disappeared in the more explicitly sexualized culture of the 1960s, there was still an enduring expectation that individuals, if they were fortunate, would meet the man or woman of 'their dreams' and go on loving them until the unimaginable age of sixty-four. By the beginning of the 1970s it had become acceptable, throughout the West, for heterosexual couples to live together without the blessing of either church or state, and – increasingly – to leave each other if love disappeared. An orthodoxy (albeit contested) developed which argued that divorce and separation were better for children than long-term disagreement between their parents.[25] With this, and part of this, was the acceptance of the idea of marriage and long-term relationships as essentially matters of consumer choice, in which individuals had the right to leave

20

unsatisfactory relationships. It was feminists who pointed out the structural inequalities of marriage, but they did so in a culture which was already losing its belief in that particular form of relationship.[26] The feminist badge 'Don't Do It, Di', at the time of the royal wedding of 1981, was designed as a comment on the institution of marriage rather than Diana's unfortunate choice of partner. In this emphasis feminists alluded to an older tradition of thinking about marriage than that of Diana: a tradition which recognized that marriage involved individuals but also had a known history of turning individuals (men, women) into the different people of husbands and wives.

By the late 1980s Charles and Diana had played their part in helping to discredit the very ideology of romance that had initially united them. Scepticism about romance is no new thing, but the royal couple helped to revive that traditional wariness ('marry in haste, repent at leisure') about romantic fantasies that had always been part of our culture. In this it has often been difficult to refuse romance, or romantic love, since to do so seems to embrace a cold-hearted attitude to others that is seen as chilling and dismissive of others and individual difference. We have needed romance, since without it we are faced with the prospect of admitting to certain material and physical needs which it is often more psychologically comfortable not to address. The characters in fiction – and real life – who have admitted to their material motives in marriage have been regarded as basely calculating. To say of someone that they married 'for money' or 'security' carries with it a negative association: that person becomes a 'gold-digger' and as such worthy of public condemnation. We have come to expect love and romance in marriage and/or long-term relationships. It is, for Western people generally, a sign of the superiority of our culture that we do not associate marriage with explicitly material or social convenience. We no longer assume that heterosexual sexual relations have to be regulated and organized through marriage, but we do expect that marriage is constructed through love. Thus whilst

21

we have taken marriage out of love and sexuality, we have not taken love out of marriage.

At the beginning of the twenty-first century we thus pursue 'love' with unstinting enthusiasm. We want to be loved, and to love, and the word, and the expectation, is used generally and frequently throughout our culture. It is – as the following chapters will suggest – a word with diverse meanings. We have been told that 'Love means never having to say you're sorry' and Prince Charles has told us that although he used the word he had no idea what the word meant. Yet we use the word endlessly in everyday conversation and in written communications. It is a word used to influence, to indicate a particular position and to initiate actions. We love ice cream just as much as we might love our cat or the person with whom we live. We are, as people in our culture – very active as 'lovers' of objects, situations and even people. But the extent to which the same word is used to cover a multitude of possibilities should also warn us of the conceptual confusion around the idea. It is possible, therefore, that we love too much and too widely and that we have reached a situation where it is difficult to distinguish between different kinds of love, and the different contexts in which we might love. In this confusion we may no longer be able to distinguish 'true love' or 'real love' from matters of taste or inclination. It is equally possible that we never could and that it does not matter if we no longer make these distinctions. The argument here will be that current redefinitions of the meaning of love have become more open about the distinction between sexual desire and love, but are deeply confused about the links between love and morality. We are more able than previous generations to live our personal lives without threat of unwanted pregnancy, economic dependency and the social stigmatization of the unmarried, but a new moral order has yet to emerge. The theoretical fascination of love (apart from its endlessly seductive personal appeal) is its potential for both creation and destruction – a potential recognized by societies from the dawn of history. The question to be asked in the following pages is thus about the state of health of 'love' at the beginning of the twenty-first century: is it a redundant concept in a secular, sexually liberalized society or does it still exist, and should we encourage its existence, as a necessary, passionate assertion of our humanity against the calculative normality of late capitalism?

In considering these questions there are three issues which will recur throughout the discussion. The first is that of the relationship between love and desire. Centuries of romantic poetry and passionately expressed romantic feelings attest to the capacity of human beings for loving each other. The look across the crowded room (for example, in Tolstoy's *Anna Karenina* the moment when Vronsky sees Anna and 'the blow falls') and the sudden recognition of the desired other have long been portrayed as 'love at first sight'. Science might tell us that we are smitten for biochemical reasons, but we assume that we have encountered 'love'. The more sceptical might suggest that we have seen a sexually desirable person: this is not 'love' but lust. But a feature of our contemporary Western culture is that we do not have to decide: we can desire and we can love. This raises a second issue which will recur here – not our freedom both to love and to desire but our moral confusion about how we do this. We have, to a significant extent, separated sexuality both from marriage and from the dominance of heterosexuality. Welcome though this may be, it nevertheless raises questions of how – if at all – we should now organize personal relations. The deregulation of sexuality is, for many people, an attractive option, given those long histories of the persecution and the harassment of the sexually nonconformist. Yet the absence of moral regulation may not involve the sexual anarchy of fevered imaginations but the dissolution of desire and eroticism. Laws (in the sense of customs and conventions rather than formal legislation) about sexuality may not threaten it, but actually underpin and maintain the force and power of the erotic.

23

The final question which must run through any account of love is that of the relations of women and men to love. One of the most important features of the Enlightenment was to assume the possibility of human domination over Nature. However, the identification of women with Nature bequeathed a complex legacy of the relationship of women and men to love and desire, in which women have had to reclaim a voice for female sexual desire: we now appear to have reached a point where the Western social world does not formally distinguish between the engagement of women and men with love and desire. We still need to consider if a discourse of equality allows discourses of difference.

2

Going Back

This is the use of memory;
For liberation – not less of love but expanding
Of love beyond desire, and so liberation
From the future as well as the past.
                    T. S. Eliot, *Little Gidding*

On that hot day in July when Lady Diana Spencer became
the Princess of Wales she and her husband, with all of us
as active or passive participants in the marriage ceremony,
took part in a ritualized form of personal commitment
whose structure had not changed since the seventeenth
century. Marriage, as we know it in the West, has been the
predominant form of the social recognition of 'love', so
much so that the 'right' to marry remains a goal for those,
most particularly gay people, at present excluded from it.
Marriage, and getting married, still exercises a powerful
hold on the public imagination and even if we are likely
to divorce as well as marry (and cohabit) we are still, in
Britain and all of Western Europe, very unlikely not to
marry if we have children. Increasingly, it would appear
that many people experience a triple reality of personal
relationships: a period of cohabitation when young and

childless, marriage when older and when children are born, and possibly a time of divorce and living alone. To many pundits, moralists and politicians, this appears to be the making of a new (and unwelcome) moral order, but whether it is actually this, and not the most recent manifestation of an older pattern in which pre-marital sexual relations were often tolerated, marriage was entered because of pregnancy and ended by death, is a matter for conjecture.

There is – as the change in heterosexual relations becomes associated with what is supposed to be a 'crisis' in the family – no shortage of sociological literature on the question. From this literature what emerges – at least in the case of Britain (and the rest of Europe) – is actually a picture of relative stability in family relationships, in which many children grow up with their natural parents and in which supportive relationships between generations are maintained.[1] More of an issue here, however, is the question of the meaning of love, the understanding and assumptions which people bring to that crucial emotional 'glue' which makes and breaks personal relationships. The concern of this chapter, therefore, is the history of 'love' in the West in the past 200 years. The questions which we then need to ask about 'love' are questions about how 'love' has changed, if that is the case, and the extent to which 'loving', in a sense once understood, is no longer either required, esteemed or possible.

One of the many 'love troubles' of the West has always been that we have never been (in just the same way as Prince Charles) entirely sure what we mean by love. Histories of love typically assume that 'love' is always located in the context of heterosexual relationships: for many of us 'love' began with the famous lovers of medieval Europe, was articulated more fully – and more clearly within the context of Christian marriage in the seventeenth and eighteenth centuries – and then became rather more diverse, and complex, in the nineteenth and twentieth centuries. The rediscovery and the rewriting of the history of sexual and emotional relationships between people of the same sex has led – in the past thirty years – to the recording of the 'lost loves' between gay people, between siblings and across class and gender lines. The love that 'dare not speak its name' no longer suffers any such inhibition and writers such as Terry Castle, Lillian Faderman, Liz Stanley and Carol Smith-Rosenberg have all celebrated the intense loves between couples who did not accord with conventional expectations.[2] The impact of this literature has been to demonstrate and articulate what many people have always known (and is recorded in many historical records) that love is, as is said in English folk-wisdom, both blind and a very funny thing. We all know of people who 'love' outside the boundaries of human, adult life: people whose love for their pets, their children or their train sets is infinitely greater than any love for adult human beings.

Love, we have to acknowledge, has always been confused and confusing. It is typically spoken of in metaphors of illness and disease: a feeling which 'infects' and 'disturbs' the orderly presentation of self. Yet the paradox of love has also been that it can bring both order and chaos and make and break relationships. For centuries it has been recognized that love can heal, repair and succour just as much as it can destroy and damage. But these complexities and contradictions of love fit badly with much else that is characteristic of the twentieth century, in particular the extension of what Max Weber described as the 'iron cage' of bureaucratic control.[3] Part of this process – and part of the very meaning of 'modernization' – has been the elimination and the attack on those aspects of social life which have seemed to represent pre-scientific and 'irrational' patterns of thought. 'Love' is part of this confused (and often confusing) aspect of our lives and from the eighteenth century onwards we have tried – as citizens of a post-Enlightenment, scientific culture – to make 'sense' of love. Hence, we must ask if we have done this.

At the end of the eighteenth century there emerged, in England, two contradictory sets of ideas about the nature of love. On the one hand was the definitive statement by Jane Austen of Enlightenment morality: love could be understood and was as much a matter of rational thought as it was of passion and sexual desire. Austen recognized different forms of love than those of heterosexual marriage (for example powerful love between siblings) and she also recognized – more clearly than most of her predecessors and her successors – the ease with which sexual desire and love are confused. Against this account was the romantic view, voiced by Shelley and others, that love, most often equated with sexual desire, should always be spontaneous and never controlled or structured by social norms. 'Love is free', wrote Shelley: 'to promise for ever to love the same woman is not less absurd than to promise to believe the same creed.'[4] These different positions on love set much of the debate about love for the nineteenth century: on the one hand was a morality which only associated love with heterosexual marriage, on the other a consistent, and powerful, veneration for romance.

The literary meeting of love, romance and marriage which is most familiar to many people is Charlotte Brontë's great saga of erotic enslavement, *Jane Eyre*. The novel was published in 1847, written by an author critical of Jane Austen, and yet in many ways as disciplined and sceptical of romance. In her novels Austen had set out a critique of romance which remains still pertinent: the silly girls of Austen's fiction who fancy themselves 'in love' are as much part of the twenty-first as the early nineteenth century. Nor is (or was) Austen alone in her critique of the romantic: there has been a consistent opposition between those who try to construct personal love as something other than sexual desire (whether heterosexual or homosexual) and those for whom sexual desire (the 'I want you' of popular song and fiction) *is* love. Individual experimentation with different sexual partners and different sexualities is now possible publicly in a way which it was not 200 years ago. The West has cautiously allowed new forms of romantic partnerships (between people of the same sex most particularly) and has dissolved the previous tie between love and marriage. Charlotte Brontë's *Jane Eyre* ends – like the work of many of her contemporaries – with marriage. 'Reader, I married him', has become the by-word for studies of romantic fiction. This closure suggests, like the ending of the novels of Jane Austen (and to a lesser extent the fiction of Elizabeth Gaskell and George Eliot), the end of individual problems. Marriage, in this fiction, is the resolution of individual lives and the point at which love takes on a social and institutional form. Writing of adultery, Tony Tanner has described marriage thus:

> Marriage, to put it at its simplest for the moment, is a means by which society attempts to bring into harmonious alignment patterns of passion and patterns of property; in bourgeois society it is not only a matter of putting your Gods where your treasure is (as Ruskin accused his age of doing) but also of putting your libido, loyalty, and all other possessions and products, including children, there as well. For bourgeois society marriage is the all subsuming, all organizing, all containing contract.[5]

Although the novels of Austen and Charlotte Brontë both lie within the form of society to which Tanner is referring, there is nevertheless a shift in attitudes between their work. Austen, for all the twentieth-century interpretations in film and television serialization which have translated her work into tales of romance, remains a true product of Enlightenment rationality and is deeply opposed to the romantic. Her work is scattered with highly dismissive comments about people who 'fancy' themselves in love or who marry on the basis of physical attraction. Thus in *Pride and Prejudice* the endearing (but essentially absent) father Mr Bennet had allowed himself to become 'attached' to the rather less intellectually gifted Mrs Bennet because of her youthful charms. In contemporary language, Mr Bennet 'fancied' Mrs Bennet and because of this condemned them both to a lifetime of ill-matched marriage. Without for one moment referring to his own disappointments,

Mr Bennet makes it plain to his favourite daughter Elizabeth that to marry without respect for the other party is a very poor recipe for domestic contentment. In the same novel the hero Darcy speaks (or writes) of his sense of having become 'irrational' in his love for Elizabeth. He does not say of himself that he is proud to have been swept away by strong and romantic feelings (or an intensely charged eroticism); on the contrary, he speaks of having lost control of his feelings: as he says in his letter to Elizabeth, 'I was not then master enough of myself to know what could or ought to be revealed.'[6] In that same letter, part of which Darcy writes in order to explain to Elizabeth his strong feelings against Mr Wickham, Darcy uses an expression about his sister which occurs elsewhere in Austen. Explaining to Elizabeth that Mr Wickham had attempted to persuade Georgiana Darcy to elope with him, Darcy says of his sister than she was 'persuaded to believe herself in love'.[7] What this remark contains is an understanding of both the power of romantic love to initiate action and its limited basis in rational understanding of either the self or the other party. 'To believe' oneself in love is not to think or reason but to accept a state of being separate from rational discussion and demonstration.

Elizabeth and Darcy (like the other heroes and heroines of Austen's novels) eventually negotiate a marriage which is based on both mutual attraction and mutual recognition. That this is not always achieved is recognized very fully by Austen. The case of Elizabeth's parents is provided as a warning (appropriate to both young men and young women) that youthful good looks are not necessarily the same as enduring human qualities. But Austen is not one-sided in her portrayal of physical attraction: Elizabeth Bennet herself is attracted to the personable Mr Wickham. Even if she does not approach the silliness of her sister Lydia, for whom every man in an officer's uniform is immediately attractive, she is nevertheless far from immune to the charms of handsome young men. Silly, romantic girls are a staple part of Austen's world and all of them have to learn that both their physical attractions and those of their potential partners are fleeting and limited. No character in Austen is allowed, through the conventions of the society of her world, to enter into an acceptable sexual relationship outside marriage, and so the courtship rituals in Austen are those of conversation and behaviour in public, rather than performance in private. What is important here is to disabuse ourselves of our contemporary idea that those characters in Austen who confused love and sexuality would have made better choices in a different moral and sexual climate. Lydia Bennet might not have married Mr Wickham in the late twentieth century (and no doubt they would have enjoyed a great deal of active sexuality) but there is no reason to suppose that the relationship would have been any more successful today than in the past. The problem, if this is the right description about the relationship of Lydia Bennet and Mr Wickham, was not the force of a repressive sexuality but the essential limitations of understanding and behaviour of the two characters.

To suppose, as some writers have done, that Austen inhabited a world of discreet gentility, is demonstrably incorrect. Her own experience involved the knowledge of imperfect and unhappy marriages, jealousies and passions.[8] Equally, the fictional world which she created is marked by her knowledge of the power of love and desire to disturb and to rule human actions. Austen knew perfectly well that real people (just as much as fictional ones) could be made ill and unhappy by imperfectly realized and fulfilled love. When Marianne Dashwood falls ill in *Sense and Sensibility*, we know, as Austen does, that she is unwell (and has a 'fever') because her body is bearing the burden of her disappointment about Willoughby. We see, in *Mansfield Park*, that Fanny Price grows physically stronger as she becomes more sure of her place in Edmund's affections. Above all, in that novel we see the most brilliantly realized portraits of the manipulative possibilities of love, and it is an important comment on our contemporary

31

attitudes to love and physical desire that *Mansfield Park* is often supposed to be the most difficult or unpopular of Austen's novels. Yet what that novel provides is a definitive critique of the ideology of romance, at the same time as it provides a rich understanding of the origins of love itself.

Alasdair Macintyre has described Jane Austen as the definitive moralist of the post-Enlightenment period.[9] His account of that statement inevitably includes a discussion of *Mansfield Park*, although his focus is the question of responsibility and moral choice. Another aspect of *Mansfield Park*, and one which is important here, is the way in which Austen recognizes the ways in which 'love' can be constructed and manipulated, and how close it is to sexual desire. When Maria Bertram makes a determined (and successful) effort to marry the unattractive (but rich) Mr Rushworth, she does so by dancing with him at a number of balls and through this physical association marking him out as her own. Maria is beautiful, and acknowledged as such. Mr Rushworth is neither intelligent nor handsome, but he *buys* beauty for himself when he marries Maria. Maria, on the other hand, can find neither intelligence nor beauty in Mr Rushworth and it is the clever, articulate, formidably emotionally literate Mr Crawford who engages both Maria's heart and her intelligence. What Henry Crawford can do, as has been the case for endless other fictional seducers of women, is talk to them and construct a fantasy world outside the confines of the everyday world of patriarchal control. Unlike the silent (or conversationally limited) other men in *Mansfield Park*, Henry Crawford knows how to appeal to women through speech. This verbal intercourse gives to women the promise of relationships that transcend the limits of gender: Henry Crawford is unquestionably masculine but also able to transcend the limits of conventional masculinity: he can talk about horses and hunting but he also has a receptivity to the written word that distinguishes him from other male characters. Thus whilst Sir Thomas Bertram and his younger son Edmund regard, and use, language as a form of verbal contract, Henry Crawford is open to the possibility of the ambiguities and multiple interpretations of the world made possible through language.

Unfortunately for Maria Bertram, Henry Crawford's ability to charm women with his verbal eloquence is not matched by his ability to sustain the relationships which he creates. Austen obviously recognizes, in *Mansfield Park*, the imprisonments of gender, in that she knows that judgement, rationality and inquiry are qualities which all human beings are capable of but are too often expected only of men. At the same time she also knows how even the most self-aware and morally secure individuals can be capable of the confusion of a need for intimacy with the reality of the other person. Edmund Bertram admires, and longs for, Henry Crawford's charming sister Mary, but we – as readers – are allowed to speculate that what he sees as liveliness is often nothing more than an intense engagement with the minutiae of the social world. More striking still, Fanny Price cannot remain impervious to the charms of Henry Crawford. In this relationship both come to see that her refusal of him is also her engagement with him. As Henry acquires a carapace of more appropriately conventional behaviour, so Fanny is able to step outside the shell of passive conventionality which she has constructed for herself. In both these relationships (but most particularly in the case of Henry Crawford and Fanny Price) love is being formed out of the weaving together of need and desire. That neither of the relationships succeeds (and that, in the end, Fanny marries Edmund) is due to the intervention of regulation: at moments of truth neither Mary nor Henry Crawford can recognize convention and morality.

Austen writes, in *Mansfield Park*, of the world which Michel Foucault was to theorize, and his claim about the world of the early nineteenth century is that it was a world becoming committed to the surveillance and the regulation of sexuality.[10] This obviously suggests a sense of previous societies as unregulated, and even if we must recognize that this formulation is not part of Foucault's work, it has certainly become part of some recent histories of sexuality and morality.[11] Any study of any Western society from the sixteenth century onwards demonstrates that sexuality was everywhere regulated and controlled. But this regulation was often – and here again Austen is crucial – in the hands of men rather than women and premised on the need to maintain socially recognized paternity and the economic support of women. The step forward which Austen makes is to claim the rationality of women and to suggest that sexuality (and marriage) can be conducted in a way which allows both sexual desire and rationality. As we have seen, in the years after Austen it becomes less difficult to allow heterosexual desire: effective contraception and liberalized sexual moralities can make that possible. What is much more difficult is to combine sexual desire and rationality and even to allow that it might be appropriate to relate them, rather than to regard them, as we have increasingly come to do, as unrelated states. Thus Austen suggests to us that we can find in the rational, and rational discourse and understanding, desire. To adapt the famous comment by Descartes: I think, therefore I love. To put this in another way, because you allow me to think (and to reason), therefore I can love you. The relationships in Austen which are based on physical attraction do not succeed, but nor do those relationships based on a fantasy of perfect harmony and intimacy. Marianne, in *Sense and Sensibility*, is most typical of characters (both in real life and in fiction) who use objects (and tastes) in the external world to achieve a sense of harmony with another person.

The novels of Jane Austen, with their unshrinking commitment to reason (and its difficulties) have often been seen as essays on convention. That they are not (and that Austen is deeply and radically unconventional and sometimes hostile to aspects of conventional society) should be apparent to any reader.[12] Although Austen's fiction always ends in the closure of marriage, the range of the novels, in terms of both class and emotional possibility, is far greater than allowed. What conservative readings of Austen refuse to see is that she resisted the values and dictates of a market economy, poured scorn on romantic love and had no respect for social hierarchy *per se*. Indeed, throughout her fiction Austen endorses achievement rather than ascription and rational and independent thought. Recognizing the strength of the social world, she is able to suggest possibilities of resistance to the seductive attractions of wealth and privilege. This is hardly an attractive message for a society – that of England in the early nineteenth century – anxious to find a form of social order which would allow it to escape from the awful possibilities of revolution and social upheaval. Austen recognized – and all her novels explore this idea – that a form of social contract had to be worked out in which the demands of the market economy did not become the only, or the dominant, values of the social world. The questions of love and marriage may at first seem some way from this concern, but they are closely related in that it is through individual resistance to the cash nexus that community and consensus can be preserved. To marry for money is the personal equivalent of a commitment to the prioritization of financial gain; to marry for romantic love is to marry in the midst of illusion and the refusal of those very responsibilities – of thought and reason – which are socially, as much as individually, essential.

Austen is, in many ways, hardly a comfortable novelist, even if the past 200 years have seen determined attempts to make her work acceptable and palatable to tastes which long for a pastoral and nostalgic version of the English countryside. To writers who were her immediate successors she offered what many felt to be an excess of discipline: most famously Charlotte Brontë revolted against what she described as the 'neat borders' and the 'ladies and gentlemen' of Austen's world.[13] Both Charlotte – and her sisters Anne and Emily – chose to turn to romance and fantasy for their characters and their subject matter. Charlotte Brontë's *Jane Eyre*, a novel widely read by schoolchildren, is a novel so deeply imbued with metaphors of sexuality that it is scarcely surprising that it was thought to be, at the time of its publication, a deeply shocking work. What shocked some sections of the Victorian public about *Jane Eyre* was Charlotte Brontë's refusal of respect for social hierarchy: when the young Jane Eyre throws a book at her unkind cousin John Reed and resists the authoritarianism of the Reverend Mr Brocklehurst, she metaphorically asserts the right of women to independence, and most particularly to an independence of thought.

Yet apart from the obvious critique of conventional religion and conventional morality which Charlotte Brontë offered, what she also presents to readers is a passionate hymn to romance and to the possibilities of relationships of transcendence and fusion. Jane Eyre, the apparently quiet and studious heroine, meets and captures the imagination of the older and richer hero, Mr Rochester. From their first meeting, at which Mr Rochester, in a moment of physical incompetence, falls off his horse, the pair embark on a tussle for power and control of the sexual agenda which was unparalleled in English fiction since the time of Richardson's *Clarissa*. The two speak to each other about masters and slaves and about the fantasy figures that they represent to each other. They do so in a language which is rich in suggestions of ownership, control and dominance.[14] When the discovery is made about the existence of the first Mrs Rochester, Jane flees from Rochester, only to find herself at the home of yet another controlling male figure, St John Rivers. This time, however, the man of the house does not wish to control only Jane but also the religious practices of the Indian subcontinent. St John Rivers's mission – like that of other evangelical Christians of his time – is to take English culture to other parts of the world. St John Rivers, who proposes a marriage of convenience to Jane, wishes to civilize the unknown masses whilst himself embarking upon a dehumanizing marriage.

It is at this point in the novel that Jane finally allows herself to follow her own inclinations and desires: she returns to Rochester and in the final chapter we leave them married, and the parents of a son. If this sounds too happy an ending for a novel which had dealt with the subjects of bigamy, colonial exploitation, insanity, institutional cruelty to children and endless ordinary deceit, we need to remember that Rochester has, by this time, been severely mutilated. Jane returns to an enfeebled and helpless man, no longer the lord and master of Thornfield Hall. The ending is conventional in that a marriage concludes the novel, but what is more important is the way in which Charlotte Brontë has both vindicated romance and at the same time organized romance so that it is not controlled by men and patriarchal interests. Jane and Rochester meet as romantic partners through shared fantasies, and they both allow the other party to share and enter these fantasies. As the dream of marriage fails, and Jane is confronted by the presence of Mrs Rochester, it is Jane who asserts the importance of a socially recognized relationship with Rochester – that of marriage – rather than an individualized, essentially secretive relationship, which is all that Rochester, as a married man, can offer Jane.

When Jane refuses to become Rochester's mistress, she steps out of the romance in which she and Rochester had been living and into the reality of relations between women and men in England in the first half of the nineteenth century. That reality was not one in which romance always played a central part. Increasingly, all social classes endorsed the idea of mutual attraction as a basis for marriage, but this idea was heavily qualified by interests particular to special social classes and identities. For the tiny minority of the population who owned significant wealth, to marry within that elite group was regarded as essential. To step outside it, to marry into other social classes, was almost unheard of. Penniless women may have fantasized about marrying wealthy men but – outside romantic fiction – this simply did not happen. Marriages, then as now, took place *not* across class and ethnic differences, but largely *within* them. Equally, the discourse appropriate to the formation of the marriage carried with it the marks of the particular class: the rich could afford to value beauty, whilst for other social classes more mundane characteristics of material and domestic competence had a larger place. Marriages, in the nineteenth century just as much as in the twentieth, united people with broadly similar social histories and aspirations.

The stability of the institution of marriage began to become less secure as two developments occurred in the nineteenth century. The first was that romance, as an idea and as an expectation, began to take a greater hold on the public imagination. The second was the growing public scepticism, on the part of both women and men, about the meaning of marriage. Thus just as romance acquired greater public legitimacy, so the institution which it was designed to initiate and maintain became the subject of more critical scrutiny. In England in the nineteenth century the business (for this is literally what it became) of getting engaged and getting married became a matter of increasing complexity and expense. Whereas, for example, an eighteenth-century couple who intended to marry in church might have done so by having the banns of their marriage read and then proceeding to marry and set up house, the same commitment – a century later – became accompanied (for the middle and upper classes) by engagement rituals, wedding receptions (rather than wedding breakfasts) and honeymoons. The lengthy publications which now provide details of how to have the perfect, 'traditional' wedding are informed by a practice which is barely 200 years old. Getting married had become, by the beginning of the twentieth century, a ritualized and expensive occasion. Moreover, married couples were increasingly expected to celebrate and maintain the idea of romance in their marriage: the idea of celebrating wedding anniversaries (largely unknown in the nineteenth century) had become yet another part of the expectations of the romantic, twentieth-century marriage. 'Tradition', for weddings and marriage as much as for other aspects of the social world, had been invented.[15]

The numbers of couples for whom this idealized version of a romantic marriage actually corresponded to the lived reality of domestic life is probably small. But at the same time as few people actually chose (or could afford to choose) to engage in a ritual of domestic romance, the refusal of this engagement became, for many people, a cause for dissatisfaction within marriage. Spouses who forgot wedding anniversaries could be deemed neglectful and uncaring and twentieth-century Western situation comedy made much of the case of the husband who 'forgets' romance and romantic occasions. Even though the domination of marriage in heterosexual relationships has now largely disappeared from the Western media, the importance of romance in 'relationships' still underpins much of the text (both verbal and visual) of the mass media. Throughout the West, publications such as *Hello!* and *OK* are replete with individuals in poses of romantic adoration. Even though appearing in *Hello!* has now been said to put the curse of failure on any relationship, the magazine never lacks candidates willing to arrange themselves in suitably romantic situations. As marriage becomes a more and more problematic institution, so it appears more and more possible to feed a public appetite for romance.

One of the most vivid accounts of our contemporary confusions about love, romance and marriage is Kathryn Flett's *The Heart Shaped Bullet*.[16] In the book's conclusion Kathryn Flett writes that 'Out of the nine weddings that my friend Fiona went to in 1995, five of the marriages had failed within three years.'[17] This is slightly (but only slightly) higher than the norm for rates of divorce in the United States, where it is predicted that of all first marriages half will end in divorce. Whilst Kathryn Flett's book recalls her own heartbreak at her short-lived marriage, it also recalls the seriousness and the elaboration of her preparations for it. But more than this, the book offers an important insight into ideas about love and romance at the end of the twentieth century, for Kathryn Flett can stand back from herself and view her expectations with a degree of detachment and irony:

> What I sought – a successful career, a wonderful man, perfect children, a beautiful home, inner peace, intellectual stimulation, exotic travel and knees like Princess Diana – was, I knew, at least in part an agglomeration of powerful but pernicious glossy magazine fantasies, but the fantasies were too powerful to be resisted, even by a woman who helped peddle them.[18]

And a few pages later we have a description of 'falling in love' which conjures up images of losing control and consciousness:

> For me the process of falling in love with Eric involved all the half-remembered, visceral, hurtling-down-the-roller-coaster-with solar-plexus-in-the-throat sensations; the near delirious, drugged detachment from the outside world and – pinch me I must be dreaming – a sense of having just discovered what was, perhaps, maybe, the missing piece of the big jigsaw. But despite the familiar, addictive high, I also felt as the ancient explorers must have felt when they threw away the old maps marked 'Here Be Dragons' and struck out into uncharted territory. I stumbled and, finally, fell hard and fast, but then it was never going to be any other way. And while I obviously needed him, he seemed to need me just as much. Soon we had 'Our Song' – 'Sense' by Terry Hall.[19]

Here, then, is a contemporary account of falling in love: in all respects very similar to those of previous centuries, in which the same feelings of helplessness have been re-called. 'Falling in love', to be the real thing, is assumed to take people out of their ordinary, everyday selves and locate them in some other, different space. This is not about joining with another through rational exchange or argument; this is about the abandonment of those very expectations of the rational, the sensible and the ordered.

At the same time, as Kathryn Flett says, 'falling in love' allows us to entertain the idea that the endless loneliness of human existence can be ended. The hope is that 'out there' there is the person who will understand us, comfort us and know us in a way which defies expectations of separate, adult, autonomous existence. In finding this soul-mate, this 'other', we will be able to return to that state of infancy in which we were (hopefully) part of a united mother and child relationship. Young infants cannot speak of the pleasures which they experience as part of that relationship, but if they could they might express it in the words that Kathryn Flett uses to describe the love she feels for her husband: 'For the first time, then, I had discovered the most exquisite abandonment, the ability to lose myself in someone else completely, to trust them completely.'[20]

The happy and contented infants who might pen these words about their infancy are endlessly fortunate, not least because they are less likely to seek in adult relationships what they have not received as children. It is tempting, given the ways in which falling in love is described (by Charlotte Brontë as well as Kathryn Flett) to suggest that those people whose childhoods are the most disrupted are the more likely to fall in love in ways which express the need for the completion of self. Certainly Jane Eyre tells us, in the final chapter of the novel, that she and Rochester have 'become one'. The possibility of finding through romance the other human being who can complete an individual's existence is articulated very powerfully in *Jane Eyre*, and no less so in Emily Brontë's *Wuthering Heights*. Indeed, in these novels what is established is a powerful fictional agenda for romance which has yet to be overturned. Although Charlotte Brontë (just) situated *Jane Eyre* within the discourse of conventional marriage, Emily Brontë did no such thing, and for her this institution was a block rather than a step forward to personal happiness.

In *Wuthering Heights* we have the definitive discussion of the possibilities, and the impossibilities, of transcendent heterosexual love. When the young Catherine makes her famous declaration ('I am Heathcliff'), she also parodies conventional expectations of romance in the account she gives of her feelings for Edgar. The restoration of harmony at the conclusion of *Wuthering Heights* is achieved through marriage, but it is a marriage formed without the conspicuous needs and passions of other relationships in the novel. The tale of Catherine Earnshaw and Heathcliff is neither happy nor fulfilled, but the endless appeal of the novel (or the idea of the novel) is that desire, in its negative as well as positive sense, is recognized and articulated. At the time of the publication of *Wuthering Heights* various interests in Victorian England were attempting a greater regulation of marriage and sexuality. From these attempts no single consensus about marriage and sexuality was to emerge (indeed the fragmentation of the normative order on the subject of heterosexuality was to begin at the end of the nineteenth century); but what did achieve a fixed place in the public mind was an idea of romance, and indeed the legitimacy and validity of its existence. More problematically, just as the idea – and industry – of romance took its place as part of the normative order of industrial capitalism, so the material basis of relations between the sexes started to shift. Slowly at first, but with increasing public recognition, another idea took place alongside that of romance: the idea that marriage should be a relationship between legally and socially equal partners. The 'problem' in these two changes was that the expectations of women and men about marriage did not change in the same ways, nor did the arrangements of the public and institutional spheres about marriage.

To the great English women novelists of the nineteenth century (Jane Austen, the Brontë sisters, Elizabeth Gaskell and George Eliot) the idea of a marriage without love and mutual respect is abhorrent. Of the tradition, it is the Brontë sisters more than the other women who uphold the possibility of transcendent heterosexual love. For the other authors, marriage is to be negotiated in other ways. One of the ways which all the authors endorse is a shared sense of social values: these women bring into the private spaces which they create in fiction a sense of the relationship between the public and the private. Contrasts here can be particularly acute: we have little idea about Rochester's politics (although we have to suppose that he has a less than socially progressive attitude to non-white people) but we have very specific information about the politics of Thornton in Gaskell's *North and South* or Ladislaw in Eliot's *Middlemarch*. What both these authors do is to suggest a social contract as well as a personal contract in marriage. The marriage formed in *Middlemarch* between Dorothea Brooke and Will Ladislaw is about the achieved congruence of the social and the personal. These relationships are not only about 'romance' (even if we are told that they offer individual fulfilment to the parties concerned) but are also about the social meaning and context of personal relationships. In contrast to Mrs Ladislaw and Mrs Thornton, Jane Eyre, as the second Mrs Rochester is left, literally, isolated in her romantic marriage.

Fiction by women in the nineteenth century sets out, with little sentimentality, the possibilities of marriage and romantic love. As the nineteenth century gave way to the twentieth, however, fiction increasingly articulated the tensions and strains of marriage. In *The Bell Jar* Sylvia Plath memorably recreated the choices for women by the end of the first half of the twentieth century: choose marriage and children and choose with it domestic isolation and dependence; choose autonomy and remain childless and socially marginal.[21] But what Plath also articulated, very forcefully, was the battle for control of the agenda about heterosexuality between men and women. Plath wrote at a time (*The Bell Jar* was published in 1963 but is set in 1953, at the time of the execution in the United States of the Rosenbergs) when a particular form of suburban domesticity was held to be the most desirable form of human existence. The 1950s are as complex a decade as any other, but in them – particularly in the United States and to a lesser extent in Britain – frequent and articulate

instances arose of what the historical record would suggest is a long-standing dispute between male and female
interests about the nature of love and marriage.

This dispute – which in the twentieth century largely
took the form of the expression, by men, of the sense that
marriage was a 'trap' and, by women, that men's only
interest in marriage was access to sexual relations – has
been expressed in a long tradition of writing by male authors. Essentially, the tradition – which dates from the end
of the nineteenth century – asserts that masculinity is being threatened by two features of industrial society: the
increased independence of women and the demands of
bureaucratic industrial society. D. H. Lawrence best illus-
trates the first tradition (as do H. G. Wells and Arnold
Bennett), whilst Sinclair Lewis and George Orwell epi-
tomize the second.[22] In a later generation John Osborne's
Jimmy Porter expressed the furious rage of both himself
(and his author) when he railed against the demands of
domestic life.[23] But it is not merely domestic life *per se*
against which this tradition rails: it is the sense of domestic
life as yet another form of bureaucratic control. In *1984*
Orwell suggested a link which remains widely canvassed
in Western societies, that the future, the 'modern', is in
some sense destructive of emotion. In doing this, Orwell
largely endorses the view that the social organization of
the kind necessary for the efficient functioning of complex
industrial societies carries with it the constant threat of a
loss of human individuality and those human emotions of
love and care. Large-scale organizations, be they private
companies or societies, have no place for the person, or
the expression of individual difference.[24]

Ideas about the dominance of bureaucratic organization
were part of Western thinking at least thirty years before
Orwell. The idea of the 'organization man' (literally such
given the gender segregation of the labour market) reduced
to a cipher by all-powerful bureaucracies is part of the
fiction and the non-fiction of the 1920s and 1930s. Sinclair
Lewis captured the empty life of the white middle-class

employee of the United States in *Babbitt*, just as Charlie Chaplin did for the factory worker in the film *Modern Times*. Lewis's *Babbitt* was published in 1922 and pre-dates by some seventeen years Orwell's *Coming Up for Air*, a novel in which he rehearsed some of the themes in *1984*. All these novels (and Chaplin's film) share a perception of the future as a place in which individuals become dehumanized by the demands of the workplace (and come to think and act in the terms of the market place) but are saved, or attempt to save themselves, by love and romantic encounters. Love as redemption thus becomes a prevailing motif in all these encounters with modernity: men saved (or trying to save themselves) from the incursion of the values of the market place by turning towards an alternative set of priorities. In this search the gender politics of the 'flight to love' are consistent: Babbitt's wife, like that of George Bowling in *Coming Up for Air*, are as deeply implicated in the values of the alien world as their husbands. It is the 'other' women, the women outside the marriage, who represent freedom.

In this we have to ask if male writers of the twentieth century (in this case of fiction but not necessarily only in writers of fiction) come to associate women – as wives – with the same intrusive dominance as the bureaucratic organizations for which they work. The organization man (George Bowling and Babbitt) thus come to dislike not just their wives, but the personal bureaucracy of the home and the household, with its routinized expectations and aspirations. Both the hero of *Babbitt* and that of *Coming Up for Air* see themselves as oppressed by the domestic ambitions of their wives. Even though the men themselves are deeply involved in their own agendas of consumption, they nevertheless carry with them a sense of burden about the needs of their wives. Women, it is clear in the works of Lewis and Orwell, have become part of an onerous system of domestic oppression. From biographical and autobiographical material by and about him, we know that Orwell had little sympathy for the demands of domestic life, even though he was always enthusiastic about the experience of it.[25] In common with many middle-class men of his generation, he had little experience of domestic life except as organized institutionally or by women. Throughout his life, Orwell turned to women (most particularly his wife and his sister) for domestic support.

This pattern of the gendered responsibility for the household and domestic life is not, as a considerable literature demonstrates, one which is confined to either the twentieth century or the middle class. Orwell was nothing if not typical in his assumption that women managed the private space. That he was more ambivalent about this than he realized is apparent in *1984*: in that novel he is demonstrably hostile to the idea of the collectivization of domestic life, yet at the same time is critical of what he sees as the slipshod and slatternly housekeeping of the 'prole' wives and mothers. His praise in his non-fiction as much as in this fiction, is for the 'good' wives and mothers who maintain, often in the face of considerable hardship, a well-ordered domestic world. Orwell did not accommodate himself easily (either in his fiction or in his own life) to the twentieth-century emancipation of women. His fictional solution to the transformation of gender relations implicit in the changes that took place in the situation of women (particularly economic emancipation and autonomous control of fertility) was to construct romance, and to find, in the idealized fantasies of romantic engagement and transcendence, a resolution of the tensions that could not be negotiated in reality. The wish to resolve tensions in relations between the sexes is hardly a unique phenomenon of the twentieth century. For a brief period – at the end of the eighteenth century – there had appeared – in Austen – a sense of the possibility of a genuinely rational engagement between men and women, but the development of a powerful industry and ideology of romance increasingly obscured the rational – for both sexes – in constructed expectations about 'romantic' behaviour. Men in romantic accounts of 'being in love' had to be ardent suitors, whilst women were expected to be bashful maidens. There was little ideological space for female heterosexual desire or for the uncertainties and ambiguities of either sex.

In *1984* Orwell named the 1960s as the decade in which the old world gave place to the new world of Oceania and Big Brother. For many people the 1960s occupies precisely the same place as it does for Orwell in *1984*. The 1960s are widely identified as the decade in which the 'permissive society' arrived throughout the West. If this new form of society did not literally wipe away the past, as happened in Orwell's novel, then it transformed both expectations about, and the institutional context of, love and sexuality. In all Western societies (if at slightly different times) divorce became more widely available, as did contraception and access to abortion. Homosexual relations were decriminalized for adult males and a new politics of sexual identity became part of the political map of Europe. Evidence about the degree of *actual* change in individual sexual behaviour before and after the coming of the 'permissive' society is inevitably inconclusive, in that accurate material about sexual behaviour is notoriously difficult to collect, and by virtue of the very transformation of public discourses about sexuality it is likely that previous patterns of sexual behaviour would be more likely to be acknowledged. But what can be seen in reality is that the discussion of sexuality (in both its physical and its emotional implications) became more open and more specific. Homosexual relationships became more widely tolerated, and expectations about pre-marital chastity virtually disappeared, as did expectations about the absolute and necessary relationship between pregnancy and marriage. In the 1950s Doris Day had sung with confidence, and an apparent absence of public irony, that 'love and marriage go together like a horse and carriage'. By the end of the 1960s popular music took a rather more aggressive and sexually explicit attitude to love, whilst marriage (apart from the endlessly failed marriages of country and western music) had more or less completely disappeared as a context for love and romance. The times, as Bob Dylan pointed out, had changed.

Attitudes to the 1960s demonstrate a multiplicity of different views about the changes, both personal and general, that took place in the period between the mid-1960s and the mid-1970s. To the socially and politically conservative the decade did herald a decline, a set of negative changes which were directly responsible (and are still blamed some forty years later) for the decline in family stability, promiscuity and a general, if rather less specific, sense of declining standards. (The standards which are supposed to have declined as a result of the permissive society range from scholastic abilities, most often cited as a decline in basic literacy, to inter-personal manners and behaviour in public.) To the less socially conservative, the 1960s were a beginning to the end of hypocrisy, the absence of personal freedoms and – especially for women – a decrease in patriarchal control. Even those feminist voices which have argued about the relatively greater appeal and value of the permissive society to men, rather than women, accept that some of the institutional constraints on women's behaviour were very rightly abolished in the 1960s and 1970s.[26]

The reasons for the shift in values in the West in the 1960s and 1970s are various, but not least was the growing economic emancipation of women, an emancipation which coincided with the shift to a new form of Western capitalism – a form based on the service sector and personal consumption. One of the great, and resonant, phrases of the 1950s is Richard Hoggart's description of the emerging world of the consumer society – 'welcome to the candyfloss world.'[27] That image, with its association of the fairground and the ephemeral, conjured up much of the same sense as later more lengthy discussions of consumption.[28] This new world was one of intense, immediate, gratification and did offer to the population as a whole a share in what was to become a global village of delights. Access to consumption became more general, not simply because more people acquired more disposable income, but because there was more to consume which was generally available. The 'mass consumption' which so frightens Orwell in *1984* had become a reality by the end of the 1970s, and with it a world in which many of Orwell's fears (particularly about surveillance and the nature of mass production) were apparently only too real. In this new world of Western consumption people had not been reduced to the terrified slaves who people *1984*, but the pressures to consume, and to be able to participate in a world in which *consumption became a form of social integration* had become considerable.

Concern about the impact of the 'consumer society' is no new thing. For example, in the 1930s the decline in the birth rate in Great Britain had become the subject of earnest debate by social scientists.[29] Richard Titmuss, amongst others, had spoken about the emergence of a world in which women and men chose to remain childless rather than embark on the costly exercise of parenthood. *Parents Revolt: A Study of the Declining Birthrate in Acquisitive Societies* (which was published in 1942) voiced concerns about the social impact of voluntary childlessness.[30] Titmuss advocated more aid by the state for the support of children and mothers, but part of his argument also lay in concern about the appeal of consumption (as A. J. P. Taylor described it, the 'appeal of the Baby Austin rather than the baby in the pram') over the joys of parenthood.[31] This concern was largely forgotten in the post-Second World War rise in the birth rate, and has remained largely dormant since. However, what has now replaced this concern, at least in Great Britain, is the high rate of teenage pregnancies in Great Britain (the highest in Europe) and fears about the gradual erosion of two-parent families. For a significant minority of children the reality of family life is now life with their mother, whilst for adults (of both sexes) without children the increasingly common pattern of adult life is that it will be lived alone. In our concern with these phenomena, we have tended to overlook two things: first, the fact that the stable family life we assume in the past was as much disrupted by death, migration and poverty as contemporary family life is by divorce; and second, that family life is intimately linked with patterns of consumption and the demands and expectations of the wider social world. However much we would like it to be, the family is not a 'haven in a heartless world', in the phrase used by Christopher Lasch.[32] On the contrary, the family is, for some people, the place from which they escape, rather than the place they escape to. For example, in her study of the intersection of family and work life, Arlie Hochschild found that many people considered the regulated world of work far more personally rewarding than the unregulated world of the household.[33]

It is in the light of this evidence that we have to ask how, if at all, the contract between the sexes is being re-negotiated. In his account of sexual relations in the West in the late twentieth century, *The Transformation of Intimacy*, Anthony Giddens has argued that what he sees emerging in the West is what he describes as 'confluent love', a form of love between the sexes which is not necessarily located within marriage, but is essentially (Giddens argues) democratic in that both parties recognize the rights and demands of the other party.[34] As Giddens says:

> The possibility of intimacy means the promise of democracy . . . The structural source of this promise is the emergence of the pure relationship, not only in the area of sexuality but also in those of parent–child relations, and other forms of kinship and friendship. We can envisage the development of an ethical framework for a democratic personal order, which in sexual relationships and other personal domains conforms to a model of confluent love.[35]

Giddens does not underestimate the difficulties of fulfilling this ideal of personal relationships: as he says, there are 'deep psychological, as well as economic, differences between the sexes', which stand in the way. But he remains confident that what can be achieved is a situation in which male and female people can live together in harmony, however limited the extent of the duration of that harmony.

The evidence of history and contemporary information suggests that in couples where there is some approximation of social power and income the possibility of confluent love exists – and has always existed. However, what Giddens tends to assume is that the social and material status of both parties will be adequate rather than inadequate and that each party will be a fully participant member of the educated, high-skill economy. Should the parties not be part of this section of the population, then the chances of confluent, democratic love are probably as great, or as limited, as they ever were. Historical and biographical evidence suggests that in circumstances of material need relationships of love and care were constructed, but that all too often the old folk adage 'When poverty comes knocking, love flies out of the window' was a rather more accurate account of domestic relations. In short, what Giddens assumes as the basis of confluent relations is a degree of prosperity and economic independence.

For those materially assured individuals of the contemporary world there is – as Giddens rightly points out – no reason to relate to others through strategies arising from dependence and fear of material insecurity. Both women and men can (and in some cases do) act as economically autonomous beings, for whom sexual relationships are a matter of choice rather than necessity. The fly, or flies, in this picture of possible contentment are the costs (both financial and otherwise) of children and of economic misfortune, through unemployment or redundancy. In the first case – the arrival of children – it is well known that children are extremely expensive in Western societies in that they limit the potential earning power of women and involve high costs for maintenance and education. All calculations of the cost of a child now include the loss of the mother's earnings. Even if the mother returns to paid employment (a strategy usually involving part-time work for most mothers and much more popular, and possible, in Great Britain than in other European countries), then income has to be assessed in relationship to the cost of child care. The arrival of a child thus returns our couple of late modernity to the constraints of a previous era: an era in which marriage was specifically designed, protected and maintained in order to ensure the material survival of mother and child.

Every individual in every Western society is now familiar with the slogans that surround recent changes in the situation of women: 'you've come a long way, baby' and 'having it all'. Women, it is supposed, have emerged from the dark confines of the domestic world into the light and free space of the public world. Just as the Queen of the Night (the person who in Mozart's *The Magic Flute* embodies the forces of the irrational) was defeated by the forces of reason and enlightenment, so we are asked to believe that these same forces have allowed women to step out into full citizenship and social participation.[36] Women, it is argued, can 'have it all' (in the sense of combining, in the same way as men have always done, paid employment and parenthood). Indeed, it is now argued that the pendulum has swung too far 'in favour' of women, and that the gains of feminism, for middle-class women, are such that it is men (and working-class women) who are now the more disenfranchised and under-privileged. There is as yet little real evidence (other than hearsay impressions about life amongst a metropolitan middle class) to demonstrate that anything has shifted the power base of white, middle-class men as rulers (if not owners) of the planet, but the view has been clearly articulated by writers such as Ros Coward and Susan Faludi that there is now an identifiable and substantial crisis of masculinity affecting the West.[37] Coward and Faludi do not see, like Giddens, greater democratization in relations between women and men, indeed part of their argument is that there is growing inequality (in favour of women) between women and men. What all three writers agree on is that the domestic contract between women and men, particularly in the white, educated middle class, has been rewritten since the 1960s, and largely as a response to the changes emerging in those years.

In the work of Anthony Giddens on love and intimacy (and indeed in the work of Ulrich Beck and Elisabeth Beck-Gernsheim) there are fleeting appearances of that phenomenon described by Margaret Thatcher as fiction, namely society. All three writers acknowledge that human relationships do not take place in a vacuum; nor do they conclude, like Margaret Thatcher, that only individuals, their families and the state exist. But what is problematic in the work of all three, just as much as is the case for Coward, is the nature of the relationship between 'society' and the individual. Society, in the sense of a shared culture, is part of the context in which we all live and work, but society is also part of, and related to, the particular economic system of capitalism. It is often argued – and with increasing frequency in the past twenty years – that the world in which we live is 'postmodern' and that we are citizens of modernity (or late modernity) rather than capitalism, but the tendency of capitalist social relations to intrude upon our lives remains marked. Thus the capitalism of the twentieth century shifted its needs from unskilled to skilled workers, and towards increasingly complex technology. For the great majority of people their existence is determined by the place they can obtain, and maintain, in this new labour market. Making this point is to emphasize the importance of recognizing the context in which individuals conduct their personal lives: we may think and feel that we are 'free' when we make and initiate personal relationships but our freedom to make these relationships, and certainly the quality of them, depends upon our standing in the public world.

That public world, of paid work and civic engagement, is now arguably becoming not more democratic or more socially equal but more unequal and less democratic. Thus we have to consider not only whether the analysis of personal relationships offered by Giddens is correct but whether or not the world outside those relationships is not developing *structural* characteristics (in the location of social power, the growth of economic inequality and the discrepancy between the prosperity and the stability of the North as opposed to the South) which both inhibit the possible democratization of intimate relations but also actually discourage it. Indeed, a more likely account of contemporary intimate social relations is that what is being produced (through shifts in patterns of employment) is an increasingly unequal society in which a few people, both men and women, may enjoy the democratic possibilities of social and material privilege, whilst the rest of the population is increasingly vulnerable to the two most destructive challenges to stable and fulfilled intimate relations, namely economic need and ideologies of romance. In this, of course, we see the essence of Orwell's prediction for the future coming true: a small minority able to enjoy the transparently visible riches of the global economy, whilst the majority is subject to endless economic need and an ideology of highly sexualized individual intimacy. The media industries offer a form of inter-personal intimacy which is dependent upon the achievement of identities created through participation in consumption. Here the 'candy-floss' world creates its own participants, participants who can fully engage in society only if they are effective as consumers. But to be an effective consumer demands a commitment to, and engagement with, the labour market which may marginalize other activities and priorities. The 'time poor' individuals of late capitalism are then ideally suited to fleeting romantic encounters but much less so to long-term relationships which may demand the investment (to borrow from the language of the market place) of time and effort.[38] When Ulrich Beck and Elisabeth Beck-Gernsheim formulated the idea of 'the Normal Chaos of Love' they suggested that love is always disorderly and chaotic. A contrary view would be that whilst our behaviour when 'in love' might be occasionally chaotic, our expectations and experiences of love are very predictable and continue to follow an ancient pattern of expectation, anticipation, achievement and varying degrees of disappointment or delight. What is now more chaotic is our morality about love and sexuality: the disappearance of a widely endorsed (if not practised) fusion of love, sexuality and marriage has opened up new possibilities about the explicit separation of love from sexuality, and sexual relationships from marriage. We still assume marriages to be formed through love, but the internal personal satisfactions of marriage (or relationships) have become the criteria for its continuation rather than any structural constraints. Love, we might argue, is now more clearly encouraged and endorsed than at any time in its history by a social culture of entitlement and personal fulfilment. Yet, paradoxically, the power of love to reward and enrich is diminished because it is no longer associated with constraint and prohibition. The boundaries of love do not have to be those of rigid legal and social norms: this is not an argument for a return to authoritarian interventions in marriage and sexuality. But it is the limits of the idea of the 'pursuit of happiness' which might demand our attention.

3

The Language of Love

Mr Rushworth was from the first struck with the beauty of Miss Bertram, and, being inclined to marry, soon fancied himself in love.

Jane Austen, *Mansfield Park*

He had listened to so many speeches of this kind that they no longer made any impression on him. Emma was like any other mistress; and the charm of novelty, gradually slipping away like a garment, laid bare the eternal monotony of passion, whose forms and phrases are for ever the same.

Gustave Flaubert, *Madame Bovary*

In England, in 1960, the word 'fuck' was officially allowed, in the words of Richard Hoggart, 'to escape into free print'.[1] The event which permitted this extension of the range of the written word was the prosecution of Penguin Books for publishing an 'obscene libel', namely the unexpurgated version of D. H. Lawrence's novel *Lady Chatterley's Lover*. Hoggart, himself called as a witness for the defence, has described the event as 'intellectually dramatic' and a moment 'at which the confused mesh of

British attitudes to class, to literature, to the intellectual life, and to censorship, publicly clashed as rarely before – to the confusion of more conservative attitudes'.[2] To date the 'permissive society' from November 1960 is to over-simplify the changes taking place throughout British (and North American) society in the late 1950s. Nevertheless, the acquittal of Penguin Books allowed the English public (whether as writers or readers) to move towards sexually explicit written material. (Later battles were to be fought over similar boundaries in the theatre, the cinema and visual arts.) The 'language of love' could now include not just a discussion of the sexual (because that has always been the case) but a naming of the body and sexual acts.

One consequence of the disappearance of controls about written language was the gradual emergence of a written culture in which individuals could advocate either the sale of their sexual services or their wish for sexual encounters. By the end of the 1960s it was possible, throughout the West, to read advertisements in the press in which individuals explicitly sought sexual encounters. 'Lonely heart' advertisements had long been a feature of sections of the press, but now language was not used to disguise sexual need or longing, it was used to make it clear. Given the disappearance of taboos about the general availability of sexually explicit material, it is now possible for people to abandon coded messages in advertisements and quite openly state that what they are seeking is a sexual partner, and a sexual partner with particular kinds of tastes. Thus both straight and gay sexual partners are sought, and apart from that distinction of sexual choice other tastes (for sado-masochism and bondage, for example) are also specified. A continuum now exists in which at one end of the spectrum individuals can seek (either through a range of introduction agencies, on-line dating agencies or press advertisements) marriage or long-term relationships, whilst at the other end of the spectrum the interests of the parties are explicitly sexual.[3] What is apparent in the range of advertisement for love, sex, marriage and relationships is that individuals have no inhibition about advertising for explicitly sexual relationships. There is no pretence in many advertisements, no coded messages or disguised preferences. There may well be indications that a social relationship could emerge from a sexual encounter ('could lead to permanent relationship' is a typical comment) but the advertisement is specifically directed at sexual fulfilment. We can now ask for what we want – sexually – without either fear of prosecution or misinterpretation of our needs.[4]

Within this sexual market place there is a wide variety of social and sexual possibility. The rich (and older age groups) can seek introductions through those agencies which habitually advertise in periodicals such as *Vogue* and the *Tatler*. Here the emphasis is about the discretion of both the agency and the clients: adjectives such as 'discreet', 'selective' and 'distinctive' fill the copy for the advertisements. The clients are explicitly referred to as 'Ladies' and 'Gentlemen' and the information collected about clients includes expectations such as higher education and public distinctions. The cost of becoming a client at one of these agencies is considerable, whereas for very much less it is possible to place an advertisement in many national or local magazines and newspapers. Within the range of the media there is, then, a form of informal specialization: advertisements in the *New Statesman* lonely hearts column stress the political views of the advertisers, whereas *Time Out* advertisers put more stress on sexual tastes and matters of individual style. Interpreting the advertisement demands careful reading: a typical selection in one edition of the *Independent on Sunday* includes a 'lady' who describes herself as both 'very respectable' and 'refined' and a man in his fifties who describes himself as both 'posh' and 'impecunious'. In order to reply to one of these advertisements, readers are invited to call a voice mail number and listen to further details of the chosen individual.[5]

At the bottom of the page on which these advertisements appear (a page which is entirely typical of other pages in the British tabloid and broadsheet press) there are also advertisements for telephone lines on which people can 'chat' to women and men. In tiny print, below these advertisements, is an advertisement for 'relationship success training'. A telephone call will – it is suggested – enable individuals to find the right partner for themselves and thereby presumably achieve emancipation from dating agencies, lonely hearts advertisements and calls to complete strangers to discuss emotional and sexual life. But in reading just one page of advertisements, in just one newspaper, what becomes apparent are two important features of the contemporary hunger for emotional and sexual relationships. The first is the inevitably blurred line in the advertisement between sexual and emotional needs, whilst the second (a closely related point) concerns the attempt by many advertisers to establish boundaries around certain aspects of their lives. Thus, for example, there are both those advertisements where men and women quite obviously, and openly, seek sexual relationships outside their marriage or stable relationship, but also those individuals who describe themselves as either 'single' or 'unattached' and want to find relationships which can be placed into compartments of their lives labelled 'sex' or 'emotional' life. This form of compartmentalization does not demand that partners become involved in often complex social relationships: the exchange is, at least in terms of its stated intentions, primarily a sexual encounter. For example, the men advertising in a national Sunday newspaper in England in 1999 wanted, in the first case, 'a lady for discreet, grown-up liaison', whilst the second sought 'a lady for discrete *rendez-vous*'. Apart from the difference between these advertisers in their use – and spelling – of the words discreet and discrete, it is apparent that both are interested in meetings with women that are entirely removed from everyday social life. The expression 'a bit on the side' which has long been used to describe sexual relationships outside formal, recognized relationships may well be, to some readers, the meaning of these advertisements. However, in assuming that what is being sought in these advertisements is sex without social and moral ties, we implicitly assume a particular morality about sexuality: not just that sexual activity should be part of established, long-term relationships, but equally that sexual relationships should be personalized. Western culture has known, and tolerated, prostitution for centuries, but it is much more difficult for the culture to come to terms with the idea that sexual relationships which are not conducted for money need not be contextualized by social and personal association. The idea of 'doing' or 'having' sex, in isolation from other forms of human communication, is one which our culture finds deeply problematic. The sense of unease about what is described as 'casual' sex is one which we can trace throughout centuries of Western history.

Some forty years after the 'trial' of Lady Chatterley, there is, in popular culture, an openness about sexual activity and sexual need which did not exist – in public and in print – before 1960. Newspapers, films and television programmes all portray sexual relationships, and characters in films and soap operas will speak openly about whether or not they have, in popular parlance, 'bonked'. Indeed, in 1999, a film called *Austin Powers: The Spy who Shagged Me* was widely and explicitly displayed throughout the West. The degree of change in the extent to which the West will allow direct reference to sexual intercourse can be illustrated by the problems which confronted the distributors of the film *Sammy and Rosie Get Laid*. When this film was released in 1983 there was a considerable furore about its title: many cinemas would not display it and the title had to change completely for release in the United States. Thus in less than two decades a further demonstrable shift in the toleration of sexually explicit language took place, a shift which was replicated in the visual images about sexuality which were allowed for mainstream audiences. The 'last taboo' (as it has been described) of the portrayal of heterosexual penetration on generally released film was broken with the granting of a British certificate to the Danish film *The Idiots*.[6]

The example of what is now tolerated in the sexually explicit film (or television programme) can be replicated in terms of public discussion and debate. The public of the entire world had access, in 1998, to the details of President Clinton's behaviour with various women. Anyone with access to a television or the internet could acquire endless information about the life of the President of the United States and one of his office workers. There was no innuendo or use of code in the presentation of material about Bill Clinton and Monica Lewinsky: acts of oral intercourse were meticulously recorded, as was every presidential examination of Miss Lewinsky's underwear. 'Access to information' and 'media freedom' had acquired a meaning (and a purpose) which few campaigners for these provisions can have envisaged. Unlike the occasion when Lytton Strachey pointed to Vanessa Bell's skirt and remarked 'Semen?', and in doing so set diarists and cultural historians busy recording a seismic shift in the openness of speech about sexuality, few commentators recorded surprise at the frankness of the discussion about Clinton and Monica Lewinsky. Numerous people, both in print and in conversation, remarked that they did not 'need to know' about the various forms of interaction in the White House, but very few people expressed surprise at the explicit naming of the actions involved. Long lists of politicians (and others in public life) who had been forced out of office by their sexual behaviour were produced (a list which usually included Charles Parnell and John Profumo) but the general conclusion drawn from the Clinton/Lewinsky affair was that the explicit discussion and depiction of sexuality was no longer taboo.

There are, of course, certain forms of sexual activity which remain condemned and outlawed (literally) in the West. Generally Western societies attempt to prohibit the distribution of sexually explicit material which involves the representation or the actual appearance of children. Thus, although children are becoming increasingly sexualized by our culture (in the sense of being constructed both

61

as sexual beings and as consumers within a rhetoric of adult sexual relationships), there is, as yet, no public toleration of the dissolution of the taboo on explicit depictions of children as sexual beings. But apart from this case, the West has increasingly allowed the portrayal of various forms of sexual activity and has provided the legal infrastructure (guarantees about access to contraception and abortion and the decriminalization of homosexuality) which allow diverse forms of sexual relationships. 'Love' – in the coded sense of sex – certainly does not any longer go together with either marriage, heterosexuality or long-term relationships.

In the light (or the darkness, as some campaigners about permissive forms of representation might describe it) of the general disappearance of taboos about the explicit portrayal of sexuality, we have to record the difficulties which this permissiveness has created for many people and ask questions about the social impact of sexual 'liberalization'. (The word is explicitly enclosed in inverted commas to suggest a degree of ambiguity about the reality of liberalization.) Radical feminists (of which Sheila Jeffreys is the most vocal) have taken to task defenders of sexual liberalization and argued that what this has in fact meant has been the extension of sexual permissiveness for men, but a loss for women in terms of the range of possible negotiations within heterosexuality.[7] 'Recreational' sex, as it has been described, and a culture which endorses and indeed valorizes the idea of sexual pleasure as complete in itself, has attracted critical attention from a considerable range of the political spectrum. Barbara Ehrenreich has argued that the impact of sexual liberalization in the United States (the culture of *Playboy* and the validity of the explicit endorsement of recreational heterosexuality) has lessened those ties which men might previously have maintained with wives and families.[8] A culture of sexual entitlement, she argues, has encouraged the loosening of traditional moral and normative behaviour. In a similar vein, Germaine Greer has taken up the argument about the impact of permissiveness on women: from a position close to that of

Jeffreys she has suggested that sexual liberation has forced (or at least persuaded) women into coercive heterosexual relationships.[9]

Greer – particularly in *The Whole Woman* – has cited considerable evidence to support her view that for women sexual permissiveness has had only negative consequences. She points to factors such as the commercial sexualization of girls (particularly adolescent girls), male pressure on women to agree to sexual relationships, and the distortion of the female body in order to meet constructed expectations of female appearance.[10] As she partly acknowledges, there are long traditions about sexual negotiation (and social constructions of female appearance) and the twentieth century is not the first point in human history when social pressures attempted to persuade women to meet male expectations. The question – for Greer and for all others who are currently concerned about the pressures on people of both sexes to 'do' sex in particular ways – is that of the extent to which these pressures and expectations are qualitatively greater and more disruptive of individual lives than in, for example, the nineteenth century. One aspect of the commercial exploitation of love and romance which is undeniably different – and far more considerable than in any previous historical period – is that of what can be described as 'love industries'.

This collective term covers a range of financially profitable activities, from dating agencies to sex tourism and from the manufacture of greetings cards to therapists whose business is the repair of emotional life. It is generally recognized that in the nineteenth century wealthy Western societies began to produce goods related to marriage and romance; cards to celebrate St Valentine's Day are the most frequently quoted example. But cards for 14 February are just one trivial part of what has now become a massive industry related to various aspects of love, sex and romance. Prostitution may well be the oldest profession, but in the twenty-first century the term 'sex industry' covers a range of activities in which prostitution is merely one part.

Within the category of 'sex industry' we also have to include massage parlours, strip clubs and sex tourism. Associated with all these is an infrastructure of publicity and publishing: 'sex work' is no longer the exchange of sexual services for money but also involvement and employment in the infrastructure of what is now a complex and global industry.[11]

The presentation of these industries has, however, remained problematic for the West, not least because those most likely to endorse the freedom of the economic market are also often those most likely to support the control and regulation of sexuality.[12] Within the politics of the presentation of the sex industry there are those who have attempted, like Hugh Hefner (the founder of the Playboy empire) to give an educated and articulate gloss to 'sex work'. Hefner has consistently presented himself as a prophet of sexual liberation, a man who genuinely wishes to emancipate Western people from puritanical attitudes to sex. Hefner, in *his* terms, is not just a man who wishes women to dress up as rabbits for the sexual titillation of men (and in doing so make a great deal of money for himself) but a man with a deep concern for the lack of sexual fulfilment in Western culture. Hefner's Playboy empire became, in the 1970s, increasingly anachronistic as more sexually explicit forms of entertainment became tolerated in the West, but what he did was to establish an important benchmark in the public discussion of the commercialization of sex – namely that this process had positive and legitimate aims. Hefner's contribution, therefore, to the sex industry was to give it a veneer of legitimacy and acceptability. Precisely because he made much of the 'rules' of the Playboy clubs (no touching or contact with the female staff), he devised a magically successful formula for Western, commercial sexuality: a formula which was grounded in the gaze of heterosexual men on unavailable women but which maintained the superiority of men as those who could look on rather than be looked at.

The discourse of the Playboy clubs had become, by the beginning of the 1970s, a worldwide phenomenon. Whilst, as suggested above, Playboy clubs were to become outmoded as sexual mores changed, what had been established through them was the idea of making women, as sexual objects, available to men within a consistent marketing package. This was no longer the random, *ad hoc* purchase of sexuality but the organized construction of a business strategy. Much is now being written about the 'McDonaldization' of Western culture (a thesis derived from the global empire of a fast food restaurant chain) but the cultural impact of Hefner's empire pre-dated that of McDonalds.[13] Resistance to Hefner was considerable: Gloria Steinem wrote a famous article in which she condemned both the ethos of the Playboy clubs and the working conditions of the bunny-girls.[14] But despite these important voices, Hefner established a model of sexuality which had important implications: he made visible the male fantasy of sexually available women and he suggested the separation of sexuality and social contracts. He did this whilst at the same time suggesting that he was articulating an equality of heterosexual sexual relations: in freeing sex from social ties he argued that he was emancipating both women and men from restrictive ties and possible dissatisfactions.

Hefner's empire, as far as anyone has so far discovered, was not involved in literal prostitution. But what he did was contribute to the acceptability of another form of sexuality of the twentieth century – that of sex tourism. This industry, which has now attracted condemnation from numerous organizations in many countries, quite literally sells the sexuality (usually, but not exclusively, of women) of people in poor countries to men in rich countries. The relationship is both simple and stark: those who can afford to buy sex do so. Most problematically, the people from whom sex is bought are young, poor and unprotected by any kind of medical or social assistance.[15] Moreover, we are increasingly aware – through the work of such writers as Edward Said and Anne McLintock – of the fascination of the East for the West, and the fantasies constructed within the West about the beauty and sensuality of 'Eastern' women.[16] We know that this fascination has existed since Europeans first established trading and diplomatic links with the East. But the long history of this relationship should not allow us to assume that sex tourism is merely the twentieth-century version of an ancient idea. Sex tourism – and Hefner's empire – are different forms of the social organization of sexuality and differ in their deliberate and calculated construction of an economic relationship.

One of Hefner's many arguments about his activities (in the days when he found it necessary to defend himself) was that a visit to one of his clubs encouraged men to 'go home and have better sex with their wives and girl-friends'. This argument suggested that after a couple of hours watching the bobbing tails of the bunny-girls the male sexual imagination would be refreshed and renewed and that Hefner would have fulfilled his function of cementing marriages and long-term relationships. Hefner as the altruistic contributor to suburban marital harmony and fulfilment was never entirely convincing, but what was important about this argument was the way in which Hefner touched upon the collective male sexual imagination of the West, and made millions of dollars in so doing. Thus without endorsing Hefner's version of his activities, what we can recognize is that he realized the importance of sexual fantasies and the part which they play in creating or limiting sexual activity. When Hefner is attacked (and usually this attack takes place under the general term of the 'commercialization of sex'), what still should demand our attention is that Hefner, and others like him, nevertheless acknowledged the existence of both the sexual imagination and the imagination of sexuality. Again, many critics and cultural historians have pointed out that the articulation of the erotic has not been one of the strengths of Western culture. But precisely because the erotic has been less explicit than in other cultures, so it was easier for individuals such as Hefner to provide a substitute for a largely absent part of our cultural fabric. That he did so in ways which are both limited and limiting of the sexual imagination is as much part of a reflection on the culture itself as it is on the specifics of Hefner's views and practices.

It is thus possible to argue that the West has been particularly porous as far as the commercial exploitation of sex is concerned precisely because the culture lacks, and has marginalized, an articulate and available erotic tradition. The pleasures of sexuality were widely and publicly recognized, and recorded, until the beginning of the nineteenth century, at which point they became increasingly socially unacceptable and unknowable. It is widely – and I would argue quite wrongly – assumed that sexuality was somehow 'repressed' in the nineteenth century. The public, legitimate, discussion of sexuality certainly became less possible, but what was everywhere in Victorian culture was a richly erotic imagination. Indeed, in reading the great tradition of English narrative fiction in the nineteenth century it is possible to discern an understanding of the possibilities of the erotic which were hitherto unparalleled in the culture, precisely because the Victorians had such a developed sense of the *power* of sexuality. The attack on the Victorians and so-called repression, which was a feature of the late nineteenth-century avant-garde, effectively de-eroticized the body and sexuality in the name of greater sexual 'openness' and 'freedom'. Thus by the end of the twentieth century the disappearance of taboos about the open discussion and representation of sexuality has created societies in the West where the erotic is no more part of the social or cultural fabric than it would be in a nudist camp: the unclothed, *known*, body provides little or no scope for the elaboration of fantasy and the erotic.

The pattern of the Western history of sexual representation suggests that Western society has been left particularly vulnerable to the development of two forms of the commercialization of sexuality: one is the growth of the more or less explicit sale of literal sexuality (as in prostitution, sex tourism, massage parlours) and the second is the sale of romance and the erotic. Both these forms of commercial activity build on absences within the culture: they may, in some instances, build upon what already exists (or what is familiar) but essentially they develop, in ways which are commercially viable, those general needs of human beings for sexual affirmation and articulation which are otherwise limited or denied. When Philip Larkin remarked that for him the most erotic word was 'unbuttoning', he made a crucial distinction between the possibility of sexuality (unbuttoning) and the available and the achieved (unbuttoned).[17] The history of sexuality in the West in the past hundred years suggests that the achievement of what might be described as the unbuttoned (explicit sexual representation and the legitimation and facilitation of sexual activity) has been achieved at the cost of the possibilities of 'unbuttoning' (the erotic). Nevertheless, precisely because the extension of the public representation of overt sexuality has been so characteristic a feature of Western culture, what has become increasingly recognized as absent is any suggestion of the forbidden or the taboo. What can and cannot be said (and seen) in public has been extensively extended, so much so that what has now become visible throughout the West is not only the commercialization of sex (in the sense of the explicit sale of sexual services of various kinds) but also the growing emergence of the construction of human objects of love in terms of ideals of consumption. This is not to suggest that physical beauty and desirable appearance have not always been valued in our culture (and others) but that the determination of what is desirable and attractive is set in terms of marketable commodities. Women writers in the past decade have put this particularly clearly. Helen Fielding's Bridget Jones (who is a fictional person) states that:

As my friend Tom often remarks, its amazing how much time and money can be saved in the world of dating by close attention to detail. A white sock here, a pair of red braces there, a grey slip-on shoe, a swastika, are as often as not all one needs to tell you there's no point writing down phone numbers and forking out for expensive lunches because its never going to be a runner.[18]

Equally, Kathryn Flett, a 'real' person and author of an account of the collapse of a contemporary marriage, writes: 'And I wasn't bothered that Eric had a boxed set of *Yes* CDs and waxed purple about numerous dirgy seventies synth-rockers (I loathed them); while I was still passionate about Steely Dan and Stevie Wonder's *Songs in the Key of Life* (he didn't much like soul). This obviously didn't matter because we both liked Oasis'.[19]

These accounts of the perception of others (in this case male sexual partners by women) have been described by Deborah Philips as part of a phenomenon she defines as 'Shopping for Men'.[20] The narratives of Bridget Jones (and other fictional characters) are part of a world in which the person is identified and understood in terms of the objects they consume. To consume, in this world, is to acquire an identity, and – as Philips, drawing on the work of the French sociologist Pierre Bourdieu, points out – an identity which locates the individual within a particular class. To quote Philips, quoting Bourdieu, 'The competition for luxury goods, "emblems of class", is one dimension of the struggle to impose the dominant principle of domination.'[21] It is unlikely that Bridget Jones, or her real-life equivalent, theorizes her choice of clothes or music in quite this way, but any reader of contemporary popular fiction (particularly the genre which is known vulgarly, if accurately, as 'shopping and fucking') will recognize the assumption by the author that personality can be communicated by personal taste and that material objects are visible, and vivid, signs of character and situation.

However, before we fall into a condemnation of twentieth- and twenty-first-century worlds in which consumption is a sign (as well as substance), we need to recall that attempting to form an understanding of other people through their clothes and their tastes is no recent phenomenon. In Austen's *Sense and Sensibility* Marianne Dashwood falls in love with the faithless Willoughby in part because he shares her taste in literature. For Marianne, expressed preferences for Cowper and Pope set the seal on Willoughby's appeal. Her other suitor, the rather older Colonel Brandon, is effectively dismissed by Marianne as a romantic possibility because he wears a flannel waistcoat. This early nineteenth-century version of the white socks or red braces so scorned by Bridget Jones are an indication that personal taste, whether in clothes or literature, matters. It is through our allegiances to material objects that we define ourselves and show others who we are. In the market place of the choice of sexual partners and in the negotiations of romance we cannot appear without giving some indication of our tastes and preferences. Thus 'love' and 'falling in love' are often described in terms which locate the emergence of that feeling in visual perceptions: 'they looked so wonderful, I fell for them instantly'. The he and the she of our affections are, on the whole, usually dressed when we first encounter them and through this providing essential information about themselves.

But it is not just Willoughby's taste in literature (or the absence on his person of flannel waistcoats) that appeals to Marianne. It is also his attitude to the natural world: an attitude which reflects her own romantic perception of nature. In *Sense and Sensibility* there is an exchange between Marianne and the somewhat phlegmatic Edward Ferrars on the subject of different perceptions of the countryside. Marianne is beginning to offer an account of a particular view when Edward interrupts her and says:

> You must not inquire too far, Marianne – remember, I have no knowledge in the picturesque, and I shall offend you by my ignorance and want of taste, if we come to particulars. I shall call hills steep, which ought to be bold; surfaces strange, and uncouth, which ought to be irregular

70

and rugged; and distant objects out of sight, which ought only to be indistinct through the soft medium of a hazy atmosphere.[22]

It is a passage in which Austen rejects what we have come to describe as 'Romanticism', an account of the natural world which sees it as embodied emotion. Marianne's understanding, at least at the time of this conversation with Edward, is one which asserts the primacy of spontaneously expressed feeling. To react, to feel, to encounter is, in her account of the world, to be truly alive and emphatically unlike those (who include Edward and her sister Elinor) who express themselves more cautiously.

Austen does not express conflicts about Romanticism in explicitly sexual terms, but what she does do is to identify the fault lines in English – and to a large extent Western – culture about the proper place of 'feeling' and 'the emotions' in social and personal life. Throughout the nineteenth and the twentieth centuries debate continued between those who viewed 'the emotions' as a dangerous collection of inclinations to be contained and disciplined and those who equated emotional life, strong feelings, sexual passion with life itself. The concept of subjecting the emotions – and particularly anything related to the sexual – to discipline often expressed itself in bizarre and absurd ways: the cold baths and bans on masturbation accompanied the rigid suppression, throughout the class structure, of any direct discussion of sexuality. 'Gentility' is often associated with sections of the middle and upper class, but as Richard Hoggart showed both in *The Uses of Literacy* and in the volumes of his autobiography, the refusal of the explicit articulation of the sexual was also part and parcel of the experience of many working-class people:

> Our puritanism made us shy about admiring the body except in certain prescribed particulars. Young lads or vulgar adults could say of a girl that she had 'a right pair of tits' or 'smashing legs'; not much more. More acceptable tributes spanned just as narrow a range. Very common were

''E's got a right chest on him', and: 'She/'E 'as a lovely head of hair'. Yet in all the body got little direct verbal attention among adults.[23]

But against this puritanism, this verbal refusal of the discussion or the recognition of sexuality, were other ways of sexual expression. To quote Hoggart again, describing an incident during the Second World War:

> As we slowly circumnavigated a tight corner between tenements we passed a cluster, two young women and two youths, obviously working class, the girls stocky and bold-looking. They knew we were off to embark. The girls then shouted at us so that we all turned in their direction, and at the same time lifted their skirts right up to their waists. No knickers. Even we could translate their Glasgow twang: 'Have a good look, lads: it'll be the last cunt you'll see for a long time.' We did not feel they were taunting us; they were being generous, animal and spontaneous, offering a bit of something which was a little better than nothing.[24]

What these two extracts show us is something that is frequently forgotten in historical accounts which stress order and coherence rather than the complexity, ambiguity and contradiction of social life. Of course we can identify, in legislation, in formal institutional responses and in the statements of the powerful and the influential, particular instances and expressions of ideas which manifestly affect individual lives. The prohibitions on abortion and contraception clearly made – and continue in some societies to make – a real impact on people's lives. Yet at the same time there exist, and have always existed, sub-texts, subversive and radical ways of thinking, and resistance to the official and the proscribed which have been both known and available. Love, sexuality and romance have all had their official, and their unofficial, histories. Ideologies about the necessity of love in heterosexual relations have often disguised sexuality, just as much as sexual responses have sometimes initiated love. The function of romance has often been to 'civilize' sexual desire: Norbert Elias has demonstrated and documented the 'civilizing' process in which we have learned to behave and conduct ourselves in ways which establish a degree of distance between a particular physical function and its social negotiation.[25] We have become accustomed to eating, dressing and 'doing' sex in ways which assume a measure of 'civilization'. To speak openly and directly of sexual desire and sexual acts is therefore described as 'crude' or 'vulgar', whereas the same desire (or action) mediated by expressions of 'love' or 'romance' suggest possibilities of discussion, conversation and negotiation.

By the beginning of the twentieth century it had become the general (if not the exclusive) expectation of people in the West that sexual relationships should be 'civilized' by an aura – at least initially and often in limited ways – by professions of love. But for a number of reasons this expectation was often found lacking by both women and men. Amongst women suspicion emerged, and was professed, that assertions by men of love were only made in order to secure sexual access to women. 'He's only saying that to get you into bed' became a commonplace remark by women in both texts and everyday conversation. For men, professions of love and romantic feelings often involved what was perceived as dishonesty, since a desire for sexual relations with women was actually what was often the case. Fears of pregnancy, of social stigmatization, an assumption of what Mary McIntosh has described as the 'natural' sexual needs of men (and this absence in women) united in a cocktail in which sexual desire became love, and desire was marginalized. The negotiations, disguises and dishonesties, were put (with characteristic acerbity) by Philip Larkin when he wrote of the 'Annus Mirabilis' of 1963 in which sexual intercourse began:

> Up till then there'd only been
> A sort of bargaining,
> A wrangle for a ring,
> A shame that started at sixteen
> And spread to everything.

Then all at once the quarrel sank:
Everyone felt the same,
And every life became
A brilliant breaking of the bank,
A quite unlosable game.[26]

Written in 1967 this poem, in its knowing cynicism about the result of the 'permissive' society, anticipates by about twenty years the emergence of consistent concern about the Western liberalization of the regulation of sexuality. That there had always been sexual behaviour which did not accord with accepted standards did not affect the views of those who essentially protested – and protest – against the apparent generalization of what is perceived as 'unregulated' sexuality. Britain has so far not seen the attempts to reclaim and re-establish sexual regulation that have emerged in the United States, but all Western societies increasingly place on the social agenda concern for the 'future of the family'. To generalize about the state of sexual morality and the reality of sexual behaviour is fraught with difficulties, but what we do have information on are the fantasies and the dreams that people have about both love and sex. Again, we have to recognize that we have not, in the twentieth century, invented sexual or romantic fantasy, but what we now have are industries and infrastructures which support and articulate our fantasies.

Hefner's, and other forms of explicit sex industries, are obviously one aspect of the way in which sexual 'needs' are met in late capitalism. So are such institutions as the *clubs échangistes* of Paris in which sexual encounters between strangers are the *raison d'être* of the establishment. (Unlike traditional brothels, they charge money for entry to the establishment rather than for the sexual services of an individual). In all these institutions, from Playboy clubs, to strip clubs, lap-dancing clubs, massage parlours and *club échangistes*, the body (and virtually always the female body) is exposed, used and exchanged for financial reward. The gendered structure of this relationship has been the subject of considerable debate and an extensive literature: suffice it to say here that it is transparently, unequivocally clear that, regardless of questions about the 'freedom' or otherwise of the women involved, it is largely men who profit, financially, from these exchanges.

But if men profit from what might be described as the sale of sex, women are more likely to share in the profits of the commercial provision of love and romance. As authors of romantic novels women can make (and have always made) considerable amounts of money. If the financial exploitation of the female body belongs to men, then the exploitation of the female psyche, through the fantasy world of romance and the romantic, belongs to women. That fantasy world now has a far greater sexual range than in previous epochs: again, the argument is not that women did not (in the eighteenth or nineteenth centuries) fantasize about bondage, or about sex with other women or groups of men, but that few texts (visual or literary) existed to meet this demand. At the beginning of the twenty-first century this absence has been met, in that any literate person can read or see a range of material which caters for a variety of sexual tastes. From the quasi-documentary accounts of women's sexual fantasies in Shere Hite to the 'bodice-rippers' of popular fiction, the desire for sexual gratification is made explicit and the possible conditions of its fulfilment discussed.[27] Any bookstall in any Western country will regularly display magazines for the reader on how to have 'great' sex. (On higher shelves, in many newsagents and bookstalls, there is even more sexually explicit material available for sale to tall people.)

The crucial aspect of sexually explicit material of all kinds is that – as many moralists have pointed out – it suggests (even if it does not explicitly condone) sex without *either* the formal regulation of marriage *or* the informal regulation of romance and expectations and negotiations about 'love'. In a culture which allows the possibility of immediate sexual access it is inevitable that ideas about love become more complex, in that 'love', at least in the context of relationships between adults, is no longer equated with the initiation of sexual relations. Sex no longer 'needs' love in this culture, although it is assumed that marriage still does. The problem, for Western culture, is that marriage, for a number of reasons, has become intensely problematic. What has largely disappeared has been described by Tony Tanner as 'the belief of bourgeois society . . . that it had effected a harmonious interrelationship of patterns of property and patterns of passion and feeling, and that it was in possession of a language that could both effectively mediate those patterns and stabilize the environment'.[28] The contract of marriage, as Tanner points out, is as old as Western civilization. But what is absolutely crucial here about love, marriage and sexuality is not the length of its history but the romanticization of marriage which begins in the nineteenth century – a change which gradually undermines that understanding of marriage which Tanner has described. Prior to this point, marriage was organized around procreation and reproduction: in order for society to exist in any meaningful sense there had to be a form for the recognition and care of children. (For the rich this obviously involved, centrally, questions of property and inheritance.) Marriage marks a transition from the potential chaos of the sexual relationships of women and men to one of order. Eros, desire, what we call 'love' is not necessary to this relationship: indeed (as Tanner points out) Western literature begins with extra-marital 'love' (of Paris for Helen) and the individuals who represent 'love' prior to the eighteenth century (Romeo and Juliet, Abelard and Héloïse and so on) all stand outside marriage. Nevertheless, marriage remains pivotal to social order, a sacrament and a contract not just with another party but with God.

However – and it is a word which barely does justice to the account of the changes which it introduces – romance emerges as the untamed child of the Enlightenment. Women, and increasingly men, assert the right and the expectation to marry 'for love': 'not loving' the putative partner invalidates the proposed contract. Yet as soon as this sentiment – the idea of conjugal love – has taken root, another voice emerges (and hence the emphasis in these pages on Jane Austen) which articulates a cynicism, a world-weary voice of caution about the meaning of 'love'. Austen knows, but she cannot say because she is writing long before Lady Chatterley, that 'love' is both confused with, and yet always entwined with, sexual desire. People, Austen also knows, want to have sexual relationships: we long for physical contact and the pleasure of the physical expression of love and desire. But initial sexual attraction is, as Austen also knows, a poor guarantee of long-term conjugal happiness. How, then, is the novel expectation of 'love' in marriage to be given a basis in something other than sexual desire? The answer which Austen provided was to elevate reason, and the rational, to the status of a necessary condition to marriage – not a social contract in the previous sense of marriage but a mutual recognition of the capacity of partners to think, and to make explicit the nature of the relationship between them. Marriage becomes, in Austen, the basis for the construction of a rational life and a rational society. It is an institution which is ideally created out of the unique capacity of human beings to think and to reason. 'I think, therefore I am', the guiding motto of the Enlightenment, becomes the statement which organizes Austen's perception of marriage, an institution in which 'love' is located in the recognition of a mutual power to reason.

Austen, like other women novelists of the nineteenth century, did not suppress or repress the erotic. Indeed, a reading of her novels can reveal many instances of erotic charge and attraction between characters. But her vision of marriage as a unity of the erotic and the rational did not survive the nineteenth-century 'loss of God' or the emergence of the bureaucratic rationality of industrial capitalism. Marriage was secularized (in that it could be celebrated outside church and dissolved by civil authority) and the increasing sexualization of marriage (made possible by effective contraception) increased expectations about the longevity of 'romance' in marriage. In this context – the context of marriage for most Western people by the second half of the twentieth century – a new goal had been established for marriage: it should be formed through 'love' and maintained by it. The problem was, and is, that sexual permissiveness does not require marriage to pre-date sexual activity, and that ancient confusions about love become more, rather than less, complicated as inhibitions about sexuality decrease.

In this contemporary climate 'falling in love' and 'being in love' acquire new meanings. Living in this climate is – as writers such as Kathryn Flett have described – often deeply painful and confusing, since individuals can construct relationships through the exchange of commercially constructed 'signs' and then discover a paucity of mutual affection. Yet at the same time as the culture is deeply encouraging towards love and romance, it is sublimely indifferent if relationships end. 'We split up' is unlikely to merit lengthy discussion, whilst divorce and separation – the dissolution of the relationship which is most often taken as the signifier of love in our culture – is an everyday occurrence. In a very real and important sense, therefore, we no longer have a language of love, in that we have deconstructed love into sex and romance whilst at the same time removing love from any close *or necessary* association with any form of social relationship. What remains is, in a sense, a homeless, emasculated word, which can be used as much on letters to acquaintances as it can to describe long-term affection.

4

The Rules of Love

Soul and body have no bounds:
To lovers as they lie upon
Her tolerant enchanted slope
In their ordinary swoon.
> W. H. Auden, 'Lay your
> sleeping head, my love'

One of the assumptions about love that has often proved particularly troublesome is the confident belief that love will prove to be self-regulating. In terms of love between individuals there are numerous clichés about the 'power of love', 'love will find a way', 'love means never having to say you're sorry' and so on. These all suggest individualized love as an emotion which seeks, in an unselfish way, the best for those concerned and is never compromised by selfish or worldly interests. Equally, love for particular ideas or associations suggests a disinterested loyalty: an ability to subordinate self to the betterment of country, politics or other allegiances. In both these contexts we use the idea of love to suggest a state of uncritical, unthinking commitment. Love is, as common parlance also has it, 'blind'.

It may be the case that love can be blind (in that being in love obscures for the person concerned the shortcomings of the other person) but the world in which the love is expressed is generally not. Other people will view the beloved with more critical eyes and deliver damning verdicts about his or her shortcomings (in the case of a person) or other manifest limitations (in the case of love for aspects of the non-human world). In the history of the West it is only too apparent that, as far as recorded society is concerned, we do not admire, endorse or welcome disruptive love. Indeed, love that appears to suggest social confusion has been viewed with great suspicion ever since Paris ran away with Helen of Troy. This may well have initiated the birth of Western literature, but the view of the event recorded in that literature is far from positive. From that point onwards, too much love, love across sexual, class or racial boundaries, and any form of transgressive love was met with disapproval in the real world and suitably unhappy conclusions in fiction. Shakespeare's Othello loved too much, Romeo and Juliet loved the wrong people, Macbeth loved the wrong ideas: in these different ways characters suggested the vulnerability of those whose hearts seemed to rule their heads.

An initial form of the management of unruly human love was to situate it outside the parameters of conventional society, at the same time minimizing the expectation of love within existing arrangements of marriage. Hence courtly love, and what amounts to a celebration of adulterous love in English Restoration drama. Then, as we have seen, ideas about where love ought to be situated started to change. Thus by the nineteenth century there is an expectation that love and marriage go together; not in itself a socially disruptive idea. But what is socially disruptive is the view that the disappearance of 'love' means the end of marriage. The inability of many individuals in many relationships to sustain feelings of romantic love towards their partners has been recognized for centuries; in the nineteenth century Friederich Engels spoke of the 'fact' of the inevitable disappearance of love, whilst in the twentieth century Simone de Beauvoir asserted that 'in men, familiarity diminishes desire'.[1] Both authors – neither enthusiastic about the conventions of bourgeois society – pointed out the difficulties of bringing together so closely romantic love and marriage.

Engels and de Beauvoir (and others who recognized the problems of the uneasy 'fit' between romantic love and marriage) suggested solutions to the problem which involved both the dissolution of marriage and the greater involvement of women in the social world. Engels clearly understood the problems of women abandoned with the consequences of romantic love – namely children – and advocated a greater state responsibility for child care. De Beauvoir, whose fiction is crowded with examples of women who have 'loved too much', offered the more personally robust advice to women of greater engagement in work and the social world. In their different ways both these voices suggested implicitly that women, rather than men, were the victims of romantic love: that if love disappeared, then it would be women who would suffer. This view exactly replicated Lord Byron's comment, at the beginning of the nineteenth century, that love was women's vocation. Men might love, and might even be passionately 'in love', but it is women – this tradition suggests – who are most committed to the view that to love, in an individualized sense, is to live. Centuries of poetry and prose demonstrate the ability of men to articulate their love (largely, although not exclusively, for women) and any number of male careers have been unmade by hopeless or unsuitable loves. Yet the difference between men and women in terms of their relationship to love is that, until very recently, men have made the rules that have established the social worlds in which we love. Modernity and the modern, with their association with the feminine and subjectivity, might have allowed a more diverse model of human interaction, but in many ways we still live, throughout the West, in societies which assume an identification of the public and the objective with men and the private and the subjective with women. It often now appears

81

– because contemporary societies depend upon subjectively established ideas of personal identity and personal taste to maintain consumption – as if the subjective is the dominant mode of human understanding, but this ignores those areas of social life (about economic power and relations between nation states) which are determined by structures and institutions. The 'rules' of social life may now allow a greater diversity in inter-personal relations, but the same constraints – of relations with the economic market place and public law – exist today as they have for generations.

The engagement of women and men with the public world has been, again for generations, very different. Hence in thinking about the 'rules' of love an inescapable part of the discussion is the impact of gendered difference on the construction and experience of these 'rules'. Patriarchal public law established rules about sexuality, sexual relations and marriage and in the main these laws served to establish both the legal inferiority of women and the need for their protection. As histories of English (and North American) law have demonstrated, the tradition of law on both sides of the Atlantic was to assume the second-class status of woman as both citizen and moral agent.[2] Women were (generally, if not absolutely) subject to the authority of fathers and husbands and supposed to be, in moral terms, less capable of judgement. In the particular context of sexual relations between women and men, it was women who were 'led astray' and 'got into trouble' by men. In nineteenth- and twentieth-century fiction authors reflected the many paradoxes and contradictions of a culture which wanted both to limit female sexual desire and at the same time admit the sexual desire of men for women. We see in Elizabeth Gaskell's *Ruth* a woman novelist attempting to rescue women from predatory men and to assert the innocence of 'fallen women'. In the same century Tolstoy and Flaubert punished those women whose passion for men other than husbands transgressed all expectations of socially appropriate behaviour. As Tolstoy makes clear in *Anna Karenina*, aristocratic society was never against adultery *per se*; its objections were to disturbance of the social order.

The social consequences of illicit and/or transgressive sexuality in twentieth-century fiction become, for women, less mortally punishing as the authority of marriage decreased. Nevertheless, until the 1960s it was still widely taken for granted that men were the instigators of sexual relations with women. In two English novels which were hailed as exponents of the new 'frankness' in literature (Alan Sillitoe's *Saturday Night and Sunday Morning* – first published in 1958 – and Stan Barstow's *A Kind of Loving* – first published in 1960) it is still the case that women cannot admit sexual desire.[3] For example, in *A Kind of Loving* the hero suggests that his wife (whom he has been forced to marry because she is pregnant by him) enjoyed sex. This brings upon his head the fury of his mother-in-law, who vehemently defends her daughter against what she describes as 'disgusting accusations against my daughter's character'.[4] Throughout the 1950s and 1960s the men who made both popular and high culture produced work which assumed the reluctance of women to sleep with men outside marriage and the determination of men to persuade them otherwise. The 'rules of the game' assumed that if women agreed to pre-marital sexual intercourse and became pregnant, then 'decent' men were expected to marry them. The 'shot-gun' marriages were the result of 'going all the way'.

Then – as the previous chapter suggested – it would seem as if the world changed. The question for us now is whether this has actually been the case, and in particular whether or not the rift between men and women about love, romance and morality is still considerable. The new morality (or absence of morality, as its detractors would claim) takes for granted an openness in sexual relations and a world in which effective contraception assumes that fleeting sexual encounters between men and women are possible without long-term consequences. 'One-night stands' carry no inevitable social consequences, whilst opportunities for transient sexual relationships feature in advertisements for holidays. For example, the film *Basic Instinct* (directed by Paul Verhoeven and released in 1992) demonstrated that individuals could radically misinterpret the meaning of sexual encounters, but no one supposed or suggested that the misunderstandings were anything other than problems specifically for the people concerned. No one was about to be whipped, branded or outlawed in this new moral world; 'unwanted' or unexpected pregnancy could be dealt with by abortion and neither lives nor careers need be interrupted.

This account of the present is, for some people, an account of what should be the case: namely, the recognition that sexual desire is often arbitrary and spontaneous and, if possible, should be recognized and organized as such. To others, this view of sexuality raises appalling possibilities, which range from the wholesale abandonment of morality to a vision of a bleak future in which sex is – in this model – 'reduced' to physical acts. A tradition in fiction (both film and prose) has, throughout the twentieth century, presented the future as a world of asexual beings, in which reproduction is either artificial or dissociated from long-term relationships. What this tradition clearly epitomizes is the fear that sexual relations actually *are* only about sex: that physical desire (whether homosexual or heterosexual) is an appetite which can be met like other hungers. From Aldous Huxley's *Point Counter Point* to George Orwell's *1984*, to much science fiction of the past fifty years, there is a general construction of the future as a world without romance and without the particularity of personal relationships which is generally thought to be characteristic of the 'real' world.

But *1984* (and *Point Counter Point*) are both novels by men and are arguably male reactions to a future which allows the emancipation of women into the public world and encourages the eradication of those differences of dress, behaviour and aspiration that have been characteristic of our society for centuries. The model for these future societies was the old Soviet Union, where state policy actually enshrined the participation of women in paid labour and disallowed the cultivation of personal taste in fashion and appearance. Other state socialist societies (for example China and Cuba) have followed a similar pattern of attempting to diminish manifest, explicit differences between women and men in the name of human emancipation and the worst excesses of the subordination of women which were apparent in these societies in their pre-revolutionary forms. The restoration of the ideal of the market economy has brought, to both China and the Soviet Union, Western ideas (and possibilities) about consumption. With those ideas, indeed an intrinsic part of them, is the articulation of explicit differences between women and men. Much of the world is thus brought to the point where debates about women, men and romance take place within a context of a global culture.

Within this global culture, argument persists less about the intrinsic value of romance, and romantic love, and rather more about the different attitudes and values which women and men bring to it. Western society has been quick to condemn what it sees as the 'arranged' marriages and the seclusion of women within a private, domestic space which it sees as characteristic of other cultures, but there has been more general resistance to the idea that, in its own terms, Western society continues to regulate love, romance and sexuality in terms of the interests and the perceptions of men rather than women. One strand in this argument is the literature which stresses the costs to women of the permissive society; another is the case, made by Carol Gilligan most forcefully, that moral reasoning is differently constructed by women and by men.[5] In a similar – although not identical – vein other women (for example Martha Nussbaum and Nancy Fraser) have argued that the central character in Western moral discourse is an autonomous man.[6] There is not, these authors would agree, an equality of moral discourse because the idea of the individual on which these discourses are based is masculine rather than feminine.

The work in which Carol Gilligan first set out fully her ideas about the different moral reasoning of women and men is *In a Different Voice*, published in 1982. This work, based on interviews with a number of teenage girls, was a critique of the psychological accounts of human development (particularly those of Freud and Kohlberg) which assumed that the human was synonymous with the male and that moral development in girls (and women) was inherently less developed than that of boys, and men. Her subsequent work (for example *Meeting at the Crossroads*, which was published in 1992) has, like *In a Different Voice*, continued the exploration of the theme of the silencing of women's voices in public debate and discussion.[7] In an interview published in 1999 Carol Gilligan spoke of her work, and her perception of the ways in which women are silenced. Speaking of Freud's account of his patient Dora, Gilligan said:

> I read the Dora case as the return of the repressed. It's the voice that Freud had to repress in order to not know women and to continue to speak in a way that would be heard and accepted. He was having enough trouble trying to speak about sexuality without speaking the knowledge that everyone was in a sense counting on silencing.[8]

The specific knowledge that Gilligan sees as being repressed and rejected by the social world is that of the recognition of the complexity of human life and human relationships. For her, what women represent and what women are concerned with is the issue of the way in which existence cannot be conducted or lived satisfactorily on the basis of what Gilligan describes as 'deadlock paradoxes'. She writes:

> What is at stake is how we love, how we work, live and so on, which has been deeply engendered, and maintained by a series of not only psychological and social arrangements but also ways of thinking. . . . The notion that the mind is separate from the body, that emotion is separate from

reason, that the self exists encapsulated and apart from relationships so that you can be in relationships and somehow hold on to your same self – all of these 'deadlock paradoxes' hold together a world-view. If that world-view shifts it means thinking very differently about the public/private split and all of those things.[9]

Gilligan's plea is obviously for a rethinking about the way in which the social world is organized, and a rethinking which integrates rather than divides the public and private. It is, on the face of it, a familiar and widely accepted view: the idea that, in the popular saying, 'circumstances alter cases' is not altogether unfamiliar in the West, nor is the critique of public, legal-rational morality as absent as Gilligan sometimes seems to be suggesting. But the radicalism of her argument is that she presents the development of different moral reasonings in women and men as part of the *ordinary* development of adolescence. In her view, it is in that pivotal stage of human development that girls cease to 'speak' and learn to repress what they already know about the world.

Exactly what it is that girls 'know' about the world which differentiates them from boys of the same age is sometimes difficult to identify precisely in Gilligan's work. *In a Different Voice* made very clear the different ways in which women and men viewed the moral issues surrounding abortion: women thought of the issue in terms of the impact of the decision (one way or another) on others, whilst men were more inclined to think in absolutist terms about the 'rights' and 'wrongs' of the decision. This difference could be interpreted – as Gilligan interprets it – as evidence of the way in which women view moral decisions in terms of their impact on others, but it could equally well be seen as an example of the way in which women, by the 1970s, had acquired a morality which gave priority to the rights of the child *and* the mother rather than the foetus alone. Moral arguments about abortion have never been static, and by the time that abortion law was being revised throughout the West the discourse about abortion was recognizably shifting towards a discussion of questions of impact.[10] This interpretation of the difference between the sexes on the morality of abortion – so crucial a part of Gilligan's argument – would suggest that what women had acquired, by the 1960s and 1970s, was a 'modernizing' agenda about questions of love, sex and morality. This agenda was much less concerned with rigid distinctions between good and bad and much more concerned with compromise and negotiation between both individuals and individuals and society.

Gilligan's study of moral reasoning in *In a Different Voice* may contain unrecognized problems, about distinguishing between the voice of women and the voice of a modernizing social agenda.[11] Equally, there may be relatively little acknowledgement in her work of the extent to which there has always been a tension in the West between women and men on moral issues – a tension in which some women have been more inclined than some men to argue the case for an understanding of the impact of the law on individuals. (The paradigmatic case to illustrate this point would be the fierce debate in England in the nineteenth century about laws on prostitution: the repeal of the euphemistically named Contagious Diseases Act marked a triumph for the voice of women rather than that of the patriarchal state.[12])

Any account of love and morality, and any discussion of what would appear to be the disappearance of different moralities for women and men, has to begin by noting the extent to which thinking about sexual morality has changed in the past thirty years. What has been described as a sexual 'double standard' did exist throughout the nineteenth and twentieth centuries and gave rise to a language about 'sowing wild oats', 'slags and drags', 'easy lays' which reflected the idea that men had 'natural' sexual desires for women which women had to resist. We also know that many women and men dissented from this morality and that it was never the only or the absolute standard. But in reading novels such as *A Kind of Loving* (or other examples of English fiction in the 1950s and 1960s) we are confronted with moral worlds which are – if not alien – at least increasingly strange. The hero of *A Kind of Loving* is a youngish man called Victor, desperate for heterosexual experience that he cannot negotiate in the community in which he lives. Since in 1960 there is little reliable contraception available for the unmarried Victor's very limited sexual activity, it ends in what is – for him – disaster, since his girlfriend, Ingrid, becomes pregnant. When she announces this, Victor's response – apart from rage at his situation – is to offer to marry Ingrid: ' "Don't worry," I said. "We'll get married. You didn't think I'd let you down, did you? You didn't think I'd take my hook and leave you to face it all on your own, did you? I'm no bloody angel, but I'm not that kind of louse." '[13] What follows is a rapid marriage, and a period of misery and disillusionment for the young couple. As Victor reflects at the novel's conclusion, he recognizes that he will never love Ingrid, but he is, as far as he is concerned, 'doing the right thing'. As he goes on: 'And who knows, one day . . . we might find a kind of loving to carry us through. I hope so because it's for a long, long time'.[14]

Within a decade of the publication of *A Kind of Loving* the public sexual and moral landscape of the West had changed dramatically. 'Forced' or 'shot-gun' marriages had become the occasions for social condemnation rather than respect and a discourse which had once identified 'unmarried mothers' now spoke of single mothers (or more evasively, single parents). The campaigning efforts of such organizations as the Brook Advisory Centre had extended the availability of contraception from the married to the unmarried and the emergence of a culture identified with young people – the 'Swinging London' of the late 1960s – had dismissed conventional ideas about sexual behaviour. By 1970 Victor Brown would have been able both to buy contraceptives openly and to question the given response of marriage to an unwanted pregnancy. These changes, furiously resisted in many quarters for a variety of reasons, would have been achieved within an ideology of personal liberation and sexual emancipation. Voices from throughout the political spectrum – for example from Mrs Mary Whitehouse – did question the idea of the separation of the moral from the sexual, but these voices were dismissed as reactionary and repressive. The new morality of the 'new' sexuality claimed an advance towards more openness in sexual relations and enhanced possibilities for the achievement of individual happiness. By 1999 it had become commonplace for films and novels to portray, without comment, fleeting sexual encounters. Women, just as much as men, could take or leave sex without any moral censure. Indeed, if Victor Brown had had a chance to visit Paris in the late 1990s he would have been able to visit those *clubs échangistes*, mentioned in the previous chapter. These establishments differ from brothels in that money is not involved in the sexual encounter and men and women enter on equal terms, with the balance of the sexes maintained by a prohibition on unaccompanied men. The *raison d'être* of a *club échangiste* is the facilitation of sexual encounters between strangers, with no expectation from either of the parties that any further social relationship will develop. To the world of Victor Brown such places would have seemed beyond the possibilities of the imagination: to an inhabitant of a world in which negotiation between the sexes for sexual intercourse was beset by a rigid regulatory system, expertly policed by a local community, the mere idea of unregulated sexuality would have seemed, quite simply, impossible. Even if relatively few people out of the entire French population frequent *clubs échangistes*, the point is that they can exist, and exist without the threat of being shut down or their owners imprisoned. Moral disapproval may be considerable, but this would no longer be sufficient to ensure – on this issue – punitive action.

The contrast that can be established between the world of Victor Brown (and other English novels of the 1960s in which unwanted pregnancies resulted in marriage or social exclusion) and that of swinging, *fin de siècle* Paris might lead us to suppose that Western societies have abandoned the attempt to police and regulate sexuality. We now assume – thanks to the impact of Foucault's work – that this was the case in the past, and a range of legislation about sexual behaviour in the nineteenth century does suggest that the codification and control of sexual behaviour was a major social impulse. But as every historian of Victorian England knows, a public normative order existed side by side with an unofficial one. Maintaining the distance between the two was energetically enforced: witness the public outcry when campaigns such as that of W. T. Stead on child prostitution or novels such as Charlotte Brontë's *Jane Eyre* demonstrated the close relationship, indeed interdependence, between 'respectability' and 'vice'. Charlotte Brontë's novel suggests to its readers that it is only through the compartmentalization of sexuality into a concealed world that the polite fictions of gentility and the absence of sexuality can be maintained. Although Victorian England was sometimes more enthusiastic in its zeal for concealment than England in other periods, this zeal did not achieve the elimination of diverse patterns of sexual engagement and relationship. This comment is made to set into context what appears to be (and is often interpreted as) the liberalization of sexuality in the second half of the twentieth century. Rather than assume that sexuality has become less rigorously controlled, we might consider that what has changed is not the nature of sexual activity but our willingness (and appetites) for its public recognition and discussion. Hence a second point about Foucault's thesis of regulation is that we should note that the process of regulation has created an impulse (which continues) for the emancipation of the body and sexuality from any form of regulation. As enthusiastically as sections of Victorian England 'saw' sex in inanimate objects or mundane everyday encounters, so they effectively, and thoroughly, hastened the sexualization of the culture. Once that had occurred, it was a small step for commercial interests to recognize the many possibilities of exploiting the newly achieved freedoms.

In the light of the above, and the generally agreed consensus that the West has, in many ways, become more open about the discussion and display of sexuality and the body, it is remarkable that individual sexual behaviour still creates such public concern. In the closing decade of the twentieth century, a President of the United States was brought close to impeachment because of his sexual behaviour whilst seemingly endless British politicians have had to leave public office because of their private behaviour. To some commentators these events are the result of a specifically Anglo-Saxon prurience: there is no evidence to suggest, for example, that politicians in France or Spain are any better (or worse) behaved. The difference is said to lie in the expectations of the public about sexual behaviour: in Anglo-Saxon countries an expectation exists that public figures will lead 'unblemished' private lives, whilst mainland European countries have no such ambitions. Quite how (or why) Anglo-Saxon countries are able to maintain their expectations about the private lives of politicians (given the record of the same) is a complex issue; here it is sufficient to recognize that these countries do still operate a set of rules and codes on what is permissable, and not permissable, about sexuality. What we can observe is that the two countries in the West (Britain and the United States) which have the highest rates of divorce also seem to be the most prone to sexual scandal in politics. It would seem that there are similarities in the culture of these countries about love, marriage, romance and sexuality which make them particularly prone to public revelation, condemnation and judgement about sexual activity. What these similarities are would be the subject of a separate study, but we might hypothesize that those cultures less willing to recognize the sexual in human motivation and action are also those most vulnerable to its complexities.[15]

What remains quite remarkable about British culture (and to a large extent that of the United States) is the extent to which individual men will go to present themselves as models of domestic fidelity and sexual 'honour'. For cultures which allow the publication and the parade of sexually explicit material there remains an extraordinary determination – largely on the part of men – to distance themselves from the suspicion of what is supposed to be illicit sexual engagement. In part this determination is closely related to that construction of men as autonomous, highly individuated social agents which was noted earlier in this chapter, but it is also part of that ancient moral agenda which assumes, tacitly, that for men romantic love and sexuality are problems, and distractions from the proper role of men, which is that of individual agency in the social world. No one expresses this view more clearly and unambiguously than Tolstoy: love for women makes fools of his male characters. Thus Vronsky, in *Anna Karenina*, abandons career and rational behaviour for Anna, whilst Pierre in *War and Peace* is so blinded by infatuation for his first wife that he cannot see her manifest failings.

Traditional, and conservative, moral agendas in the West have always articulated the view that, for heterosexual men, women are morally problematic, largely – although not exclusively – because women can make men act 'emotionally'. 'Good chaps' in the world of the Victorian and Edwardian middle class were not expected to be what is now described as 'emotionally literate'. 'Real' men did not cry, profess love or talk to anyone about their emotional states. The endless parodies of these 'chaps' – the lonely characters of Terence Rattigan's play *Separate Tables* – have now largely disallowed this social being for most of the male and female populations of the West. Men are now expected to be emotionally vulnerable and the career of the actor Clint Eastwood demonstrates how much – and how fast – expectations about men and emotions have changed. The original early Eastwood (of *Dirty Harry*, released in 1972) was a monosyllabic, sexually aggressive 'real' man; the more recent Eastwood (of *In the Line of Fire*, released in 1993) is a man riddled by emotional doubt and insecurity. Increasingly Hollywood has begun to suggest that men do not always have clear, straightforward moral agendas and that they are often beset by emotional concerns. Yet nostalgia for those agendas about sexuality which suggest that sex can be neatly organized into moral categories demonstrably lives on. In Britain, in the past twenty years, the two instances of the public discussion of the private lives of Cecil Parkinson and Jeffrey Archer demonstrate the lengths to which men will go to reinforce patriarchal codes and expectations of sexual behaviour.

The actual events which led to the public discussion of the lives of Cecil Parkinson and Jeffrey Archer were, although different in outcomes, very similar in the moral issues which they raised. Both sets of events involved the relationship of married men with women other than their wives: Cecil Parkinson with Sarah Keays, and Jeffrey Archer with Monica Coghlan. In both cases the men used the full force of English law and social power to marginalize and demonize the women concerned. Cecil Parkinson – the father of the child born to him by Sarah Keays – imposed on her restrictive conditions about the discussion of the relationship, whilst Jeffrey Archer went to court (and perjured himself) to maintain his public persona as a faultless married man. Despite the fact that it was well known in metropolitan circles that Archer had been involved in a long-term relationship with a woman other than his wife, his presentation of himself was as an ideal husband. In both cases what needs emphasis was gendered inequality in moral negotiation about sexuality. In the Parkinson case the story about his behaviour became public because Sarah Keays, pregnant with his child, refused to continue to allow the secrecy of their relationship; promises made by Parkinson to Keays were being broken. When Sarah Keays made public her account of her affair with Parkinson, the

British media readily quoted the line that hell 'has no fury like a woman scorned' and published lengthy articles about revenge and retribution. Parkinson's career was ruined and the former lovers parted in what was very bitter and public acrimony. But among the many comments (from support to Parkinson 'led astray' by Keays to support for Keays 'led astray' by Parkinson) came a comment from the diarist and Tory MP Alan Clark. Writing about a conversation with Cecil Parkinson in which Parkinson records that he will never be able to see his child by Sarah Keays, Alan Clark says: 'Cecil said he could never see the child. But what, I asked, if it was a son? He didn't reply. You would have to embrace it. You would have to go down on your knees to Ann [Mrs Parkinson], and ask for permission'.[16]

The comment is made by Clark entirely without reflection or further elaboration, yet what is made transparently explicit here is the priority of the *male* child: the child who carries the father's name and who must therefore be acknowledged and honoured. Women, in this moral code, whether they are babies or grown women, are entirely disposable: honour is a male capacity and it is not a capacity which women can acquire except through the behaviour of men to them. What separates the sexes here is moral agency: men can act honourably (or dishonourably) towards women (and the rest of the world) but women would appear to possess no such capacity. Women's lot is to remind men of their 'honour': the accusation by Sarah Keays that Cecil Parkinson had acted dishonourably towards her suggested her 'honour' was essentially reliant on Parkinson's behaviour towards her. But what we can also observe about the cases of Archer and Parkinson, and the comments on Parkinson's dilemma by Alan Clark, is the persistence of class-based codes about sexual morality. Archer and Parkinson, the lower middle-class boys whose relationship with the traditional English Establishment was always marginal, were more concerned about maintaining a public commitment to marriage than the self-styled aristocrat Alan Clark. Clark, open about his own persistent infidelity, simply took the view that his behaviour was entirely his own business.

This ancient formula, in which women's moral agency is limited to their capacity to inspire (or otherwise) the moral behaviour of men, was the moral code about love and sexuality which had underpinned sexual morality for centuries. Before the mass availability of contraception it was essential that children be protected from abandonment by their fathers: the moral code explicitly operated in *A Kind of Loving* was about the 'honouring' of children and paternity. This code largely assumed that sexual desire was one-sided: men initiated sexual relationships with women and it was therefore only legitimate that men should carry the consequences of their actions. The advent of effective contraception started to erode a part of this code: many people argued that at last women could, as it was put, 'love freely'. No doubt this was possible, but for many women the contraceptive pill also allowed the possibility of 'having sex' freely. Pregnancy could be avoided altogether and the sexes were apparently at the beginning of a new era of sexual relationships and sexual morality.

For some women this new contraceptive technology was welcomed in a straightforward and unproblematic way, but for others it created other problems about issues connected with the birth of children. The acknowledgement of the desire for children is complicated by effective contraception, in that it breaks that association between heterosexual sexuality and reproduction which has existed for centuries, and which brought into being moral codes about men's responsibility towards women. Pregnancy and children make sexuality apparent and – as Cecil Parkinson discovered – make clandestine relationships entirely transparent. We have only one-sided information about the relationship between Cecil Parkinson and Sarah Keays, but it is not unlikely to suppose that Parkinson 'assumed' the use of contraception, whilst Sarah Keays 'assumed' that a pregnancy would be regarded by Parkinson in an 'honourable' way. Contraception has, in many ways, passed the moral responsibility for pregnancy to women, whilst at the same time the social world continues to expect that men will support the children they father. Unfortunately for all three parties involved in the birth of the child, implicit assumptions about what women are doing (in the sense of contraception) are just as often unreliable as expectations about what men will do. Considerable state intervention has been organized throughout the West to ensure that men support the children that they have fathered, whilst women's refusal to accept the personal costs of unwelcome male partners has led to numerous cases of financially unsupported mothers and children. At the same time voices on the political Right (on both sides of the Atlantic) have argued that the so-called 'welfare mothers' have only themselves to blame for their predicament. Responsible women, it is argued, do not allow themselves to 'fall pregnant'.[17]

In this we can see a real shift of discourse about questions of sexuality, pregnancy and dependency. Fifty years ago the 'good' woman did not have sexual intercourse outside marriage. If she did, then it was assumed that she had been 'persuaded' into sexual intercourse by a male partner and any resulting pregnancy would be accepted and rapidly 'organized' by marriage. At the end of the twentieth century a 'good' woman is one who makes effective use of contraception, and sexual relations between unmarried heterosexual partners are acceptable so long as both are 'careful'. The technological control of nature (including the availability of legal abortion) has created a situation in which the morality of sexuality is about the use of technology and the establishment of a relationship with the body in which it is organized by what is deemed 'rational' control. The many voices raised against Sarah Keays (as frequent as those voices raised in her support) spoke of her as an inherently 'bad' girl for not recognizing that in an illicit relationship it was her responsibility to maintain effective use of contraception.

In the triangle of the Parkinsons and Sarah Keays we cannot know which person was most hurt or damaged by the affair. But we can know that almost two decades after the affair Sarah Keays has had to bring up a daughter by herself whilst the Parkinsons remain married. At a time when politicians and social scientists speak frequently of the decline of the family and the fragility of marriage it is remarkable that both Cecil Parkinson and Jeffrey Archer went to considerable lengths to maintain a particular public version of their marriages. We might assume that they did this out of a commitment to their wives and children, but we could also speculate that what they were anxious to be seen to be maintaining was the traditional moral code of patriarchal marriage in which women are either 'good' (Mary Parkinson and Mary Archer) or 'bad' (Sarah Keays and Monica Coghlan). In both cases what was being fought about was the right of men to write the moral agenda of heterosexuality: Jeffrey Archer was sufficiently determined about *not* losing control of this agenda that he was prepared to organize systematic perjury. From the court battle against the *Daily Star* Archer made a considerable amount of money, but to an already wealthy man this is unlikely to have been the driving motive. More intriguing, and more socially relevant, is the question of why Archer felt driven to fight a difficult legal battle. 'No comment' about the *Daily Star*'s allegations might have ended public speculation, leaving Mr and Mrs Archer to discuss the arrangements of their marriage in private.

However, Archer did go to court (with subsequently disastrous consequences for himself) and in doing so he drew from the presiding judge an extraordinary summing up and the use of the word 'fragrant' to describe Mary Archer. In doing this, Mr Justice Caulfield evoked one of the unspoken assumptions of a particular discourse about sexuality: that illicit sex is in some way dirty and like all dirty things, smells:

Mr Justice Caulfield told the jury they had to choose between Archer's word and that of a prostitute who had
used 'guile' and 'cunning'. After telling them to remember
Mary Archer in the witness box – 'Has she elegance? Has
she fragrance? Would she have, without the strain of this
trial, radiance? – he asked whether Archer was the sort of
man who needed 'rubber insulated sex' with a prostitute.[18]

The 'good sex' which Mary Archer personified smelt
only fragrant: this was, after all, sex in the 'right place',
the place of conventional marriage. Mary Douglas's famous discussion in *Purity and Danger* of matter out of
place was extremely relevant to the Archer libel case: the
appropriate organization of sexuality implied its placing
within patriarchal marriage and the authority of men.[19]
This emphasis on the importance of men controlling the
agenda of heterosexuality was further emphasized by Mary
Archer in her evidence. When Mary Archer appeared in the
witness box she commented that the idea of her husband
having sex with a prostitute was preposterous: 'Anyone
who knows Jeffrey would know that far from him accost-
ing a prostitute, if one accosted him, he would run several
miles.'[20] This sentence was read at the time, and most
obviously by the jury, to imply that Jeffrey Archer was a
somewhat bashful man, essentially rather frightened by
explicit sexual pursuit by a woman and the idea of a woman
initiating sexual activity. Archer's assumption, like that
of many men, is that it is up to men to be the sexual pre-
dators in relationships with women and that any departure from this order of things is entirely unacceptable. The
idea that a woman could suggest a sexual relationship
makes her immediately suspect, and liable to punishment
by the moral order of patriarchy.

The hideous spectacle of the courtroom in which two
women compete for the claim to have had sexual relations
with Jeffrey Archer is, fortunately, exceptional in the history of heterosexual relations. In this case, no one raised

issues about love and sexuality, but what was raised, repeatedly, was the question of morality. As suggested earlier in this chapter, it has been traditionally assumed that moral reasoning is a capacity more developed in men than in women. No one could doubt that through their control of public institutions men have developed a greater command of the agencies of morality, but whether or not that is synonymous with a greater capacity for moral reasoning is, as Carol Gilligan has suggested, extremely problematic. The institutions of morality (the church and the law in particular) have long been dominated by men and it is only with the development of a more openly secular society in the twentieth century that the command of morality has become more diffuse. God effectively 'died' for much of Europe in the nineteenth century, and into this moral vacuum stepped a number of alternative moral agendas for both homosexual and heterosexual communities.[21]

Not least of these agendas was that of secular love: no longer the love for God, but love for defined, existing human others. The ideology of romantic love had been part of the modernizing process of the eighteenth century and had given to women a greater degree of autonomy and choice in the arrangements of marriage. But still there remained an expectation that above all human law, and above all human aspirations, was a greater love, that of people for God and God for the world. Even if it was recognized that actual attendance at and participation in church rituals was far less significant and certainly less general in the past than is sometimes assumed, it was nevertheless the case that much of social life paid at least lip service to the idea of a greater being than human individuals. By the beginning of the nineteenth century the possible consequences of the substitution of Man for God had been recognized: Mary Shelley's *Frankenstein* is a critique of the idea that men can be God and take on the powers of an almighty being. She writes of the implications of the pursuit of knowledge:

A human being in perfection ought always to preserve a calm and peaceful mind and never to allow passion or a transitory desire to disturb his tranquillity. I do not think that the pursuit of knowledge is an exception to this rule. If the study to which you apply yourself has a tendency to weaken your affections, and to destroy your taste for those simple pleasures in which no alloy can possibly mix, then that study is certainly unlawful, that is to say, not befitting the human mind.[22]

Mary Shelley recognized long before general cognizance the moral problems endemic in the use of science and scientific knowledge. What other nineteenth- and twentieth-century writers of fiction also came to recognize was the problem for human emotional relationships of a world with pluralistic moral agendas. The simplicity of the purpose of marriage (or cohabitation) of the eighteenth and nineteenth century changed, in the twentieth century, to a far more complex and demanding agenda in which individual expectations (and aspirations) are higher whilst the actual contract is far less secure. In Europe a liberalization of divorce laws took place generally in the 1960s and 1970s, although some European countries have consistently showed markedly less enthusiasm for divorce than Britain. The United States, since the nineteenth century, has always been the world leader in divorce: a society which is openly committed to the pursuit of happiness is unlikely to put difficulties in the way of individuals who wish to maximize their individual happiness.[23] Gradually, but generally, throughout the twentieth century the idea has taken root that the end of love in a relationship is a reason for divorce. Initially, such symptoms of 'the end of love' as relations with third parties were deemed to be necessary for divorce, but this expectation has given way to a more open verdict on a marriage: that it has irretrievably broken down, love has gone and the two parties no longer wish to remain married.

In the case of relations between adult human beings with no dependent children, there is no social or moral reason why their specific domestic and personal relationships should be subject to public scrutiny: most people would recognize that all relationships (whether personal or public) should be conducted on a basis of honesty and concern for the others involved but, other than that proviso, there is no social reason why a society needs to prioritize or organize its citizens in any other way. Marriage is no longer essential for heterosexual sexual relationships and this allows freedoms and choices unknown to previous generations. It would appear that we stand, as Anthony Giddens has suggested, at a point where we can renegotiate what he describes as 'intimate' relationships and emancipate personal relationships from the control of state and church. Two problems remain, however, with this persuasive analysis. The first is that many relationships between adults involve children, whose interests are not necessarily served best by the divorce or separation of their natural parents.[24] The second is that the very fluidity of personal relationships can allow not greater freedom but greater susceptibility and vulnerability – and most of all to the idea of the possibility of the achievement of love and perfect emotional satisfaction. In short, we have acquired – for various reasons – an expectation that as individuals we can achieve states of perfect harmony with particular others: that we can return to the pre-Oedipal ideal of the infant's bliss of absolute identity with another and unequivocal love from that person. In dissolving marriage as the only context in which sexual relations and the birth of children are possible, we have also dissolved an aspirational model in which we might subordinate changing individual needs and aspirations to the maintenance of a shared contract. To honour marriage or long-term relationships is not, therefore, to honour marriage in terms of the hypocrisies of a Jeffrey Archer – with their implicit assumptions about bashful, faithful masculinity and 'fragrant' femininity – but to honour the idea that personal relationships can, perhaps, be about more than the achievement of a successfully negotiated contract or the satisfaction of physical needs. These needs – in particular the assumption of a 'right' to sexual activity – are part of a wider discourse in which God has been replaced by Nature. Belief in God always involved the acceptance of certain social rules: belief in Nature (whether about the nature of human beings or the power of natural forces) involves the acceptance of ideas of force, power and inclination both inside and outside ourselves, all of which are socially unregulated. Indeed, for many people, the appeal of 'Nature' (in the belief in the powers of crystals, the revelations of astrology and so on) is precisely that it is not part of the regulated social world.[25] The language of love has always been replete with metaphors and similes drawn from the natural world ('overcome', 'swept away', 'engulfed', are just some of the words used to describe both tidal waves and falling in love) but previous generations have not necessarily assumed that the loss of control suggested in 'falling in love' is inevitable or acceptable.

5

The Limits of Love

We outgrow love like other things,
And put it in the drawer,
Till it an antique fashion shows
Like costumes grandsires wore.
Emily Dickinson,
Collected Poems

At a crucial point in the narrative of the film *Love Story* the heroine turns to the hero, and says, 'Love means never having to say you're sorry'. The comment is made after the pair have quarrelled and the heroine is obviously telling the hero that her love for him is unconditional. The statement has been reproduced endlessly throughout the West, on cards and all kinds of other romantic memorabilia. But what is striking about this remark is the assumption that love between adults is capable of endless forgiveness and of complete acceptance of the behaviour of the other party. It is a form of love which is exactly like that ideal of love of parents for children: whatever you have done, we, your parents, will always love you. The sentiment is very far from infantile, since between parents and children it can form and maintain ties which survive severe provocation. Yet between adults, whilst we might be struck by the apparent generosity of the idea, it is also an ideal which allows both the best and the worst in human behaviour. Unconditional love between lovers can provide selfless care and support; equally, the expectation (or the aspiration) of unconditional love can underpin and legitimate abusive and violent patterns of behaviour.

This suggestion may strike some readers as harsh and unnecessarily critical of a popular, and successful, romantic film which in other ways might seem to support the values of individual affection over social convention. (The rich hero is cut off by his family for marrying a girl from a poorer family.) But the film – and its message of unconditional love – supported what we can identify as the contemporary direction and meaning of romantic love: that it is a sentiment separate from social meaning and social action. In particular, love can be separate from morality and moral expectations. For the generations who have been allowed sexual freedom there is no reason to suppose that love cannot be immediate or fulfilled. 'Falling in love' has never, for those of us who live in the contemporary West, been easier. However, whilst 'falling in love' may be easy, the next part of the song title 'Falling in love with love is falling for make believe' suggests that we might stop and consider the idea of what is now available to us as 'love'.

There are two issues with which this discussion could begin. The first is that we now live in societies which are, in terms of the availability of consumer goods, richer than any previous society. Mass consumption and production, together with the democratization of access to consumer goods, has allowed us all to have some experience (however, still profoundly limited by income) of hitherto exclusive experiences. Moreover, we can see how the very rich live by watching television and reading magazines. At every supermarket in the West we are assailed by publications explicitly telling us how the rich spend their money. 'Old money', in the sense of inherited wealth to which social status has accrued, is just as likely as 'new' money to be part of this new subject matter: Lord and Lady X 'allow' us into their beautiful home in the same way as rock stars or footballers. There obviously remains that section of 'old money' which would probably rather face the guillotine than photographers from *Hello!* or *People* magazines, but in the main 'the rich' have become a class less immediately obviously stratified into 'old' and 'new' money. (One instance of this is the enthusiasm of what is known as 'junior' members of the British Royal Family for appearing, albeit on their terms, in the mass-market press. Whether it is Lady Helen Windsor or Viscount Linley, there is a clear recognition on the part of these individuals that the only truly vulgar characteristic about money is not having any.)

We, the people and the public, are therefore now allowed into the worlds of minor royalty and successful entertainers. Moreover, we are invited to assume that our lives are their lives, in the sense that we all, rich and poor, share the common goals of a successful partnership (generally, but not exclusively, heterosexual), a 'beautiful home' and photogenic children. Even with those individuals whom we know to be many times married and divorced, we are still presented with the latest 'love' in terms which deny Dr Johnson's assertion that remarriage is 'the triumph of hope over experience'. Love can go, this world acknowledges, but it can also come again, and again. What we do not entertain, at least publicly, is the idea that for some individuals life is simply better or preferable if lived, not with one lifelong partner, but with a series of people. There is, indeed, a case for arguing that we refuse many individuals the social and moral space that would allow them 'not to love', or at least, not to have to organize their feelings and their public and private statements in terms of a discourse we call 'love'.

Expectations about the importance of love in adult sexual relationships gave individuals (and in particular women) a crucial part in agreements and negotiations about marriage in an era when patriarchal control was more explicit than today. However, since the diminution of the direct authority of patriarchy (and the advent of reliable contraception) there has been less reason for either sex to use and invoke a set of ideas about love which were derived from a different social world. At the beginning of the twenty-first century neither men nor women have to associate love with marriage, or marriage with sex, or sex with love, or desire with either love or marriage. All the once close associations of these ideas have been subverted by social and moral change. With the explicit intention of improving relations between the sexes, reformers and campaigners fought for more liberal agendas about divorce, contraception and sexuality. *Married Love* was the title of one of Marie Stopes's many publications about contraception, and even if useful information about contraception was singularly absent from the volume, the tone and argument of the book was clear: marriage should be a relationship of fulfilled sexuality and the absence of sexual inhibition.[1]

Very few people would be prepared to argue – in the name of maintaining the ideal of marriage – *for* marriages (or partnerships or relationships) which are miserably unhappy and unfulfilled. Such a possibility runs counter to the twentieth- (and now twenty-first-) century ideal of individual fulfilment and personal happiness. But at the same time as allowing that ideally marriage should be happy, we have to acknowledge that it may not be. To suppose that marriage should always be happy commits us to a treadmill of hedonistic assumptions and expectations, in which we suppose that we have to be happy (and loved) all the time. To say this, to suggest that absolute and lasting happiness is not always possible, runs counter to a culture which provides us with daily suggestions that this is an ideal to pursue. The beneficiaries of our expectations of happiness are not, unfortunately, those with whom we are most closely associated, but those nameless individuals who profit from the corporations which sell us the goods and services which will make us happy, beautiful and successful.

The argument could, at this point, take up those concerns voiced about the exploitations of the resources of our planet by a considerable number of writers. Naomi Klein has identified the seductive qualities of consumer goods in *No Logo*, whilst Richard Sennett has pointed out that changes in the labour market have led to a greater sense of individual dislocation and 'unconnectedness'.[2] The title of the book in which he argues this case, *The Corrosion of Character*, explores what he sees as the disappearance of individual characteristics of commitment and community involvement. The arguments about the erosion of a sense of a community in industrial society are of long standing and are part of the work of Tonnies, Max Weber, Georg Simmel and Walter Benjamin. All identified what they see as the erosion of control and the loss of meaning for individuals in modern society.[3] As these writers point out, the paradox of modern, Western society is that it appears to offer us everything and yet is increasingly a world without moral or cultural substance. Most significant of all, amongst a rich tradition of theoretical speculation, is perhaps Max Weber's discussion of what he sees as the 'iron cage' in which we all, in Western societies, increasingly love. This 'cage' is not one of material deprivation but it is a place in which the spontaneous is increasingly marginalized. We become 'slaves' of the market, not in the ancient sense of literal enslavement, but in the most absolute sense of both material indebtedness and moral commitment. Both as individuals and as individuals who engage with other individuals, we increasingly live in a world in which we are allowed the immediate satisfaction of our desires yet distanced from social and individual control over them.

The idea that 'having it all' and 'getting what you want' are not necessarily the foundations for human happiness was a well-defined argument by the beginning, as much as the end, of the twentieth century. In terms of the limitations of sexual conquest, and the realization of sexual desire, Freud put the case clearly in an essay he wrote in 1912 entitled 'On the Universal Tendency to Debasement in the Sphere of Love'.[4] In this essay he proposed that achieving a passionately desired sexual relationship may well be the beginning of its demise: desire is created not by the object of the desire, but by social prohibition. Freud's essay is primarily concerned with what he describes as 'psychical impotence', the difficulty that men find in achieving a fusion of the affectionate and the sensual: 'The whole sphere of love in such people remains divided in the two directions personified in art as sacred and profane (or animal) love. Where they love they do not desire and where they desire they cannot love.'[5] This comment about the behaviour of men, and the ways in which men organize their emotional worlds, must strike a chord for many women who have been involved in sexual relationships with men only to be thwarted by what they see as their partner's refusal to accept female sexuality (and desire) and to allow an equality of emotional exchange. Freud's explanation for this form of behaviour is, as he puts it, the constraints which 'civilization' imposes upon the development and the expression of sexuality. Yet, true to the ideas which he articulates elsewhere in his work and most notably in *Civilization and its Discontents*, he does not expect the absence of prohibition to bring about human sexual emancipation: 'But at the same time, if sexual freedom is unrestricted from the outset the result is no better. It can easily be shown that the psychical value of erotic needs is reduced as soon as their satisfaction become easy. An obstacle is required in order to heighten libido.'[6] So a sexual revolution in which sexual continence and the postponement of sexual relationships are rejected does not, in Freud's view, augur well for the emotional happiness of humanity. The way to achieve emotional happiness is – at least for men – suggested by Freud in the same essay, but it is a way which (as he admits) many people might find difficult to appreciate or entertain: 'anyone who is to be really free and happy in love must have surmounted his respect for women and have come to terms with the idea of incest with his mother or sister.'[7] The 'anyone' in this quotation is, of course, a male anyone, since one of the explicit implications of the essay is that it is men, very much more than women, who have problems in achieving happy and fulfilling relationships with the opposite sex. (Women, since Freud, have become vocal on the subject of why it is difficult to construct and maintain successful relationships with men. Thus, even if Freud did not fight this particular corner, it has certainly not been undefended in either the twentieth or previous centuries.)

If we put to one side, in this context, the gendered bias of Freud's argument, what remains is still important and pertinent to the way we love at the beginning of the twenty-first century. In particular two issues remain: first, the need for all individuals (male and female) to confront the issue of our desire for our mothers/fathers (sisters/brothers); and second, the relationship between the forbidden and the erotic. By the end of the twentieth century Western society had drawn aside the veil that used to be placed over behaviour in the private world of the household and with that unmasking found what is incontrovertible evidence of the sexual abuse of children and male violence and aggression towards women. It is not the subject of this essay to explore the many, complex, reasons for the sexual abuse of children, but it is important to recognize that as a culture we are still offended by the idea of attraction between children and parents and that the refusal of that idea assists, rather than inhibits, its practice. At the same time, our ideas about motherhood have tended towards the separation of maternity and sexuality: we now expect mothers to remain sexually active and attractive and as individuals separate from their children. This emphasis on separation and an almost androgynous set of expectations tends to diminish the likelihood of the resolution of the sexual and emotional ties between mother and child. The sexualization of the mother enhances the role of the mother as a sexual object, which can increase pressures and demands on mothers at a time when the care of infants constitutes sufficient work and emotional engagement. In recent years popular culture has celebrated those famous mothers who have emerged with youthful figures from the birth of children: an event of defining difference is translated into an event which is ideally of minimal effect.

What is articulated through the ways in which the contemporary West currently organizes (or attempts to organize) maternity is a congruence between the demands of the labour market and the birth of children. That congruence, as has been widely pointed out, has not been achieved and there remain considerable differences between those who wish to construct a gender-neutral labour market and those who argue that women with children neither want nor need the same kind of employment experiences as men.[8] But these literal and material factors are only one part of a twofold agenda: the other is the shift in the construction of the symbolic order of maternity and the mother: an order which increasingly sexualizes the mother and identifies the child as an object to be managed. This is not an argument against those policies which introduce nursery education or equality in the workforce, but it is an argument for the greater consideration of the impact on our emotional and sexual lives of those changes in the social organization of motherhood which we assume are about emancipation and liberation.

In the social world of the contemporary West, children are increasingly born into a culture which defines the primary purpose of heterosexual partnerships as sexual satisfaction. For many people, sexual satisfaction (in the very particular sense of the sexual rather than the sensual) is crucial to marriage (or partnership). The consequences of the birth of children to this form of relationships are often – as numerous people and much social evidence will testify – unhappy, since the relationship cannot sustain the translation of a relationship which is primarily erotic into a relationship which has to be organized around the needs of dependent others. Children cost a great deal of money and take up a huge amount of time and energy, but they are also – for many people – one of the greatest blessings of life. The question remains, however, of how our family and personal relationships can best be organized to secure the fusion of the affectionate and the sensual of which Freud wrote.

It would appear, from contemporary evidence, that for many men it is still impossible to resolve the question of desire and respect, and that individuals and corporations grow rich through providing pornography and sexual encounters to titillate male appetites. Hugh Hefner – in saying that the role of his Playboy clubs was to 'allow men to go home and have better sex with their wives' – provided a classic, textbook statement of the separation of desire and respect of which Freud wrote. There is now a considerable literature which documents the normalization of the idea that various forms of sexual encounter are essential to the maintenance of conventional marriage. 'Madonnas and whores', 'women you bed and women you wed', 'slags and drags': the ancient list which embodies the distinction of which Freud spoke continues today, but with one highly significant shift: the sexualization of marriage and the assumption of the centrality of sexual satisfaction to it.

It was Nietzsche who wrote that 'the birth of children is the death of parents'. Whilst this may have been acceptable (or simply unavoidable) to many people in the nineteenth century, it is an idea which is clearly resisted (and for material reasons very often has to be resisted) in the twenty-first century. It is apparent that our expectations of parenthood, and being a parent, have changed. A raft of evidence demonstrates that men are likely to abandon parenthood (even though successful novels and films – such as Tony Parsons's *Man and Boy*[9] – promote the case of the engaged and concerned father) and that single parents, who are usually women, are very often poor. Being a parent, particularly a father, is not expected to be accompanied by marriage and the discussion of the 'prohibitions' represented by a father (and written about by Freud) are simply fictions to a considerable number of children. The authority of the father – whether present or absent – has considerably diminished in Western societies; fathers (and husbands) can no longer exercise the absolute authority which was once reinforced by legal and social institutions.

We can, therefore, demonstrate that the social world in which the Western family is placed has changed, at the same time as the world within the family has undergone significant shifts in its internal distribution of legitimate power. We can point to social evidence which demonstrates all these changes. The psychic consequences of these changes are much harder to evaluate, not least because we cannot know with certainty what we have changed from. Nevertheless, what we can do is speculate about the emotional impact of the 'new family'. Writing of what she describes as the 'post-familial family', Elisabeth Beck-Gernsheim remarks:

> What all this means for the growing child is a matter of dispute . . . In keeping with what has been said so far, I would therefore like to propose a third interpretation. The series of events connected with separation may, that is, involve a special kind of socialization, the essence of which is a message of, and a hard lesson in, individualism. If children manage to come to terms with changing family forms, this means that they have had to learn to sever close bonds, to cope with loss. They learn early what it means to be abandoned and to part. They see that love does not last for ever, that relationships come to an end, that separation is a normal occurrence in life.[10]

Learning these emotional patterns at an early age is not, in itself, novel or confined to the twentieth and twenty-first centuries. Death, disease, famine and migration have all played their part – for centuries – in separating children from parents. Fiction, as well as documentary evidence, attests to the acceptance of practices such as wet-nursing and the 'putting out' of infants to foster parents. (For example, Jane Austen spent a considerable part of the first three years of her life with foster parents.) We would now probably regard these practices as abhorrent, but in the eighteenth and nineteenth centuries they were ways in which people with some material resources could free themselves of the care of large numbers of children.

However, the difference between the many disruptions of family life in the past and those of the contemporary world is twofold. First, the belief in romantic, transcendent love was less powerful and less generally shared; and second, the prohibition – if not the practice – of premarital sexuality assured at least a minimum of negotiation before sexual relationships were formed and the promise of intimacy suggested. People expected (and experienced) loss and death yet did so in a context of given *rites of passage*, ceremonies of betrothal and marriage which united desire with order or – as Max Weber once said in an exchange with Otto Gross – provided a formalism to save us from 'mere animalism'.[11] The sexual revolution of the 1960s (and the extensive twentieth-century sub-culture of 'affirmative eroticism') has made us all, as Elizabeth Wilson has pointed out, into bohemians:

> We no longer believe in self control and sublimation, nor do we believe that familial duty must always triumph over wayward desire. The 19th century bourgeoisie attempted to domesticate Gautier's 'modern love' but today liberal western society has gone much further in adopting what is essentially a bohemian belief in the transcendent value of erotic passion as a touchstone for the authenticity of relations between the sexes. There is a widespread belief that these relationships must be spontaneous, and marriage itself has become a celebration of that unique spontaneity between two individuals rather than a religious and contractual obligation with wide-ranging responsibilities in terms of family and property. To the bohemians we partly owe the liaison between romanticism and consumer culture in which transgression, excess and the triumph of feeling and sensation triumph over more traditionally Enlightenment values.[12]

An additional irony, which is worth underlining here, is that the very people who would hate to hear themselves described as 'bohemian', because of the word's negative associations with disruption and disorder, are now themselves adopting patterns of 'bohemian' behaviour. Those orderly citizens of Middle America and Middle England, who would distance themselves totally from any suggestion of political or social dissent, can now be found talking, and endorsing, ideologies and practices of romantic, sexualized love.

Reading (and indeed writing) material on romantic love, sexuality and desire has to raise questions for any reader or author about their own position within this complex web of needs, desires and individual emotional history. To be part of a generation (now largely over fifty) which grew up in a world of sexual prohibition (and then saw those prohibitions disappear) is to have lived through what can be seen to be a period of extraordinary social change. In 1976 my partner and I attempted to book into a large, international hotel in Madrid and were asked by the desk clerk about our marital status. On the same visit we went for a drink in a café called La Dona Liberada, in which the theme – to judge by the photographs on the walls – was the emancipation of women. The point of this anecdote is to suggest how cultures can contain – as Spain certainly did in the 1970s – elements of what seem to be vanished mores alongside more radical and contemporary ideas. In many European countries this complex pattern still exists: a gay film maker, Pedro Almodavar, directs one of the most sophisticated films (*All About my Mother*) of the past fifty years about the nature of sexual desire, in a society which retains in rural as well as urban areas rigid ideas about codes of male and female 'honour'. In Britain and the United States traditional white weddings remain popular for first (and subsequent) marriages and the structure of these weddings – in which women are 'given away' and only the men speak in the public space of the reception – has remained untouched for centuries.

Thus at the beginning of the twenty-first century, love, romance, desire, marriage and sexual relationships offer a bewildering range of possibilities to Western citizens. Definitions of marriage have extended in some parts of the West to include marriages between partners of the same sex, while the commercial market place offers sexual services of all kinds. Popular magazines contain accounts of unconventional sexual relationships ('Our marriage is happier because we now sleep with other people') and diverse sexual practices are spoken of freely on television. It is, in some ways, a bewildering display, a cornucopia of pleasure and variety that was once available to only a few people. The democratization of culture, together with the commercial interests that encourage mass culture, ensure that nobody need feel excluded from the range of information about sexuality that is now accessible. Yet what is striking about this market place of desire is the way in which love, the need and the longing for love, persists. We long to love, and to be loved and still describe our personal, sexual relationships in terms which evoke love rather than desire. Although an exception to this statement might be the explicit assertion within male homosexual subcultures that relationships can be about sexual desire *per se*, it remains the case that the idea of love, being loved and falling in love, still exercises a considerable hold on the public imagination. The 'L-word' (as Bridget Jones describes it in *The Edge of Reason*, is the longed-for seal on relationships which have already been consummated.[13]

But definitions of what love is between adults remain contradictory and often extremely close to rationalizations for behaviour that in other contexts would be unacceptable. It is this dimension of the meaning of love which is difficult for many people in the contemporary West to recognize, and in particular the use of 'love' to legitimate behaviour which could also be construed as betrayal, deceit or disloyalty. 'I really did love him' has been a mantra for those involved in illicit affairs for years: believing themselves to be 'in love' persuaded Anna Karenina and Emma Bovary to embark on their ultimately fatal liaisons. The male authors of these novels took up a stance towards their female characters which now appears punitive: Anna and Emma are ultimately more foolish and more unfortunate than the men with whom they are involved. It is clear in both novels that the authors recognize emotional and intellectual failings in men but inequalities between women and men manifest themselves in the different fates of Anna and Emma and their male lovers. Emma and Anna die terrible deaths; the men are left either untouched by tragedy (the case of Rodolphe in *Madame Bovary*) or still capable of engagement with the world (Vronsky in *Anna Karenina*). We know that the double standard of sexual morality flourished in the West in the nineteenth century, and we also know that it continued – although far from unchallenged – throughout the twentieth. What is less clear is the degree to which the double standard remains a part of our social life, even if the terms of sexual engagement have changed. One indication of the difference which persists in expectations about the behaviour of women and men is that there are few male equivalents for the role of the forgiving wife. The wives – for example Jane Clark, the wife of Alan, or Mary Archer, the wife of Jeffrey Archer – are presented as tolerant and ultimately accepting of their husband's infidelities. Most famous of all, in the past decade, has been Hillary Clinton, married to a man whose behaviour was subject to endless global examination.

All these cases – and the tabloid press provides many other examples – suggests that women remain prepared to tolerate male infidelity as a price for marriage to rich and famous men. At the same time, there are also studies such as that by Annette Lawson which provide evidence to indicate that wives, just as much as husbands, are likely to be adulterous.[14] Yet as Lawson also says, 'adultery is, indeed, firmly tied to marital breakdown' and she points out that although there are cases in which wives (and occasionally husbands) 'stand by their man' (or partner), adultery is as likely as it ever was to disrupt marriage.[15] The reason for this is the persistent relationship between romantic love and adultery: very few couples are actually 'open' about their infidelity and thus in most cases adultery involves deceit, deception and a sense of betrayal. To argue that 'open marriage' would sustain marriage (in removing adulterous relationships from webs of lies) refuses the evidence that for most people adultery involves romance and the expression of feelings of love. Once couples enter into that discourse it becomes impossible for most people to sustain marriage: saying 'I love you' to one person minimizes its validity when said to others, and partners become involved in tense, angry and destructive discussions about who loves whom, for what reasons.

These conversations, between the betrayed and the betrayer, provide the rich subject matter of countless films, novels and plays. One of the most striking quotations in Annette Lawson's study of adultery is from a member of the audience at the awards for the Booker Prize for Fiction in 1984, who said, 'I want Chinua Achebe's book to win because its the only damned book not about adultery.'[16] It is an interesting comment because it expresses much of the inevitable tedium about adultery for those not involved in it or closely associated with the participants: a third party enters a marriage, an adulterous relationship is formed and as a consequence – as the conclusion to John Updike's novel *Couples* states – 'they have been accepted as another couple'.[17] The pack of human cards is reshuffled, the furniture vans move in, and new couples emerge from old ones. At the beginning of the twenty-first century women do not have to throw themselves under trains when adultery goes wrong, and in that sense there is obviously a place for rejoicing in a greater toleration about aspects of human behaviour. Yet other accounts of adultery, and the many people for whom the only emotionally secure life is the single life, suggest that the pain and costs of adultery still persist, albeit in forms which are less dramatic than the suicides of Anna Karenina and Emma Bovary. What remains is, for many people, a lasting sense of loss and a difficulty in trusting emotional language. Writing of his own divorce (a divorce which repeated many of the characteristics of that of his father) Martin Amis described the great loss to the children of his first marriage of the end of his marriage to their mother as the fact that 'they would learn to trust love less.'[18]

Martin Amis took, like many people, a second chance on love, and it is a second chance that everyone – since we may all take the same chance – would wish well. The obvious note of caution, however, is to point out that second marriages are no more likely to succeed than a first unless – and this is crucial – couples at some point acknowledge the limitations of romantic love and their part in long-term relationships. 'Marriage' (whether literally as such or as the indication of some other form of long-term partnership between either heterosexual or homosexual couples) involves – as many societies other than that of the twentieth-century West have known – the acceptance by both parties of the limitations of romantic love. Without this recognition, the very idea which humanized marriage and emancipated women from patriarchal control becomes the idea which destroys marriage. Romantic love modernized marriage, yet it also subverts it.

At the beginning of the twenty-first century we face what is, in many ways, a more chaotic and sometimes destructive set of ideas about love, sex, marriage and relationships than at any time in previous history. We are liberated from forced marriages, from unwanted pregnancy and from thraldom to miserable and/or violent relationships, yet at the same time we are offered more complex and contradictory associations between sex, love and relationships. A previous theoretical unity of heterosexuality, romance and marriage now lies in pieces: this is not an argument which suggests that at one time all human behaviour fell into a neat, coherent pattern but it is a necessary recognition that we now have to construct our lives with fewer visible and public givens. This appears to many members of the political Right as chaotic and retrograde – 'supporting the family' becomes the mantra of right-wing politicians in the United States and Britain. Others – like Giddens, who presumably have no wish for a return to the model of personal life of the white suburbs of the United States in the 1950s – nevertheless endorse a new version of what can be described as 'secular marriage': monogamous relationships negotiated between individuals in terms of the individual contracts of the market. Where once the church and religious authority dominated, now the authority is that of the needs and demands of the market: it is not an authority which intrudes explicitly, but it is a model organized around ideas about convenience, efficiency, agreed rules and bargains. Above all, what this form of personal relationship is not is random: it is a highly deliberate and thought-out form of relationship which in many ways reproduces those aristocratic marriages of previous centuries in which the personal characteristics of individuals counted less than the other attributes which women and men possessed.

At the end of the nineteenth century the novelist Amy Levy wrote a poem about what she saw as the inevitably doomed state of marriage:

> Monogamous still at our post,
>   Reluctantly we undergo
> Domestic round of toil and rest,
>   Yet deem the whole proceeding slow.
> Daily the secret murmurs grow;
>   We are no more content to plod
> Along the beaten paths – and so
>   Marriage must go the way of God.[19]

Marriage as an institution has not yet 'gone the way of God' but our understanding and expectations of marriage have changed in the past hundred years. At the same time, we have also increasingly been allowed access to a more sexually explicit culture, and we are more subject to sexual demands and expectations. It is no longer enough to 'have sex': it is assumed that the sex will be fulfilling, exciting and diverse. In his novel about English Roman Catholics attempting to come to terms with Roman Catholic teaching about sex and sexuality in the context of secular, permissive society, David Lodge asked the question, 'How Far Can You Go?' Essentially he concluded that whilst repression made sex interesting, the absence of repression made sex ultimately tedious and lacking in interest. As one of the characters remarks: 'It seemed to Michael that he was no nearer grasping the fundamental mystery of sex, of knowing for certain that he had experienced its ultimate ecstasy, than he had been twenty years before, staring at the nudes in the Charing Cross Road.'[20]

'What will survive of us is love,' wrote Philip Larkin, in what was, for many of his readers, perhaps an uncharacteristically generous sentiment.[21] Yet while that line, quoted out of context, suggests a commitment to romantic love, in fact the poem as a whole is an argument in favour of affectionate care between individuals of the kind which Larkin also articulated as:

> we should be careful
> Of each other, we should be kind
> While there is still time.[22]

Much of Larkin's own life was spent in avoiding – or minimizing – demands by others of his time (or income). Nevertheless, he remained a conscientious son and at the end of his life assisted his long-term lover Monica Jones when she suffered a debilitating illness. Larkin recognized that he could act effectively only if he compartmentalized his life into the separate activities of work, sex, friendship and companionship. His collection of pornography allowed him to locate his erotic fantasies in – quite literally – a separate space from that of his domestic and sexual life. This profound separation of the erotic, the social and the emotional has always been possible for men in Western culture (and it has often allowed individuals to live extremely effective and creative lives) but it has generally not been an option available to – or taken by – women. However, it may very well be the case that the increasing disinclination of women as well as men to live with others is part of a growing general acceptance of the idea that the disparate emotional and social needs of individuals are met not by a single institution (that of either marriage or long-term relationships) but by the pattern of life espoused by Philip Larkin.

The acceptance and the moralization of the single – and the singular – way of life has been described by one critic of the twenty-first century as 'bowling alone'. In his study of the decline of community, and communal associations, Robert Putnam has argued that the contemporary United States has seen – in the years since the end of the Second World War – a systematic decline in the numbers of people participating in institutions such as trade unions and parent – teacher associations.[23] Putnam's argument is that the diminishing number of people who take part in these organizations reflects the disengagement of Americans from politics and government: an argument made at an earlier date by Hannah Arendt when she suggested that we have allowed the public to be swallowed up by the private.[24] Arendt's argument concerns the decline of the specifically political rather more than Putnam's, but in their different ways both authors deal with the question of the re-ordering of the relationship between personal intimacy, the family, the social world and politics – a re-ordering which has contributed little to the integrity or the vitality of any of these spheres. As the sociologist Krishan Kumar has commented:

> As the private realm of sociability contracted, the family became increasingly defenceless. Private life, now identified exclusively with the family, suffered accordingly. Private life lives off the balance, or perhaps one should say the interpretation, of public and private. By itself it strives and dries up, turning in on itself in the form of narcissism and neurosis. The predicament of private life, of the home, at the end of the twentieth century, is the predicament of our public life, emptied of meaning for all but a handful of politicians and publicists.[25]

Those remarks – and the concerns voiced by Putnam, Arendt and others from whom they are derived – are primarily concerned with the family and the structural implications for other public institutions (and of a diminished construction, and reality, of the family). But what makes many families 'fail' or fail to prosper is the lived emotional experience of individuals within those families, an emotional experience which is built out of individual expectations of love and romance. There is, therefore, a set of ideas, an ideology, at work here which is playing a part (and I would argue a negative part) in the present condition of family life. Love has been personalized and sexualized in the past 200 years and that process has been in part responsible for cutting the ties which bind the individuals to a social sense and an understanding (and acceptance) of her or his part in society. When we started to think of love in terms of romance, of sexual desire and above all of a lifelong entitlement to both experiences, then we effectively turned away from engagement with the ultimately *social* question of the impact of our actions on others. Thus we can (and obviously do) theorize extensively about the 'breakdown' of the family and the rise of the single-person society, but until we address the beliefs that motivate and inspire these changes we examine only the consequences rather than the causes of our present situation.

6

The Future of Love

Thanks to the human heart by which we live,
Thanks to its tenderness, its joys and fears,
To me the meanest flower that blows can give
Thoughts that do often lie too deep for tears.
William Wordsworth, 'Tintern Abbey'

In her account of romantic love Wendy Langford has argued that love, in the form of romance, can never give us what we desire.[1] Reviewing the 'democratization' theories of love (Luhmann, Giddens, Beck and Weeks), she points out that none of these accounts by male authors seriously or thoroughly addresses the issue of the social context in which individualized relations of love and romance take place.[2] She acknowledges that there have been studies of what she describes as the 'political economy of love', and the process through which social relations of power and domination are reproduced, but she rightly points out that the issue of power remains problematic. Langford writes:

The 'democratization of intimacy' promises liberty, equality and togetherness. In fact it is the process by which restriction, inequality and dissatisfaction are merely obscured, facilitating the most insidious government of all: government by love. . . . But contradictions within the new romantic ideal reveal it as a most unlikely path to freedom. And while quality is seen to arise from the pursuit of intimacy, men appear not to pursue intimacy at all. Women do and feel dissatisfied, yet appear keen to portray their relationships as equal anyway.[3]

Wendy Langford writes as a feminist, with a concern for the analysis of those structures, both material and ideological, which reproduce gender inequality. Her study of 'women in love' suggests that within heterosexual 'love' relationships women are only too willing to pursue relationships with men which easily become either abusive or one-sided (or both). The need to be loved drives women into initiating, and maintaining, relationships with men which rapidly give rise to those patterns of behaviour and expectation which make the continued existence or development of love impossible. To quote Langford on this point: 'Acting habitually upon the basis of unconscious fantasies, the lovers reconstruct their ego defences, reconstitute their gender identities and reproduce dynamics of domination and submission.'[4] As Langford goes on to point out, 'democratic' love does not seem to play much part in this exchange. Far from intimacy being transformed, as was Giddens's hope, intimacy seems to exist in an all too predictable and apparently unshakeable mode.

The difference between Giddens and Langford on shifts in romantic love and personal relationships is inevitably considerable, since Langford emphasizes what Giddens does not, namely structural inequalities in relations between women and men. For Giddens, heterosexual relations apparently take place in a social world in which women and men are treated equally in the world outside the home and issues such as the care of children and other dependants play little part. The real, material, evidence about patterns of caring, social power and gender inequality in income play little part in Giddens's analysis. It is absolutely correct to assume, and recognize, the transformation that has taken place in the conduct of sexual relationships in the past thirty years, but that transformation – a transformation which essentially acknowledges and assumes the importance of recreational sex and the existence of female heterosexual desire – is only a part of relations between the sexes. Equally, assumptions about the arrival of more 'democratic' patterns of heterosexual sexuality may correspond to the behaviour of urban professionals, but this group of largely childless individuals does not live in the same way as others in the population. Indeed, a brief reading of the history of sexual relations in the past 200 years would demonstrate that a small section of the population, materially rich and socially confident, has *always* been able to pursue sexual relations of relative freedom and absence of constraint. These relationships may, at times, have been constructed within a discourse of 'man and mistress' or 'wife and lover' but these organizing titles were just one aspect of relationships which were freely chosen and maintained. Both fiction and non-fiction suggest that the social world of the West, whatever its public moral hegemony, actually allowed considerable space for the unconventional and the different in personal and sexual relationships.

The impact of the sexual liberation of the 1960s was to shift public expectations about personal relationships in such a way as to suggest that the arrangements of the past about sexuality were 'hypocritical' and 'repressive'. The mantra of the 1960s was one in which 'openness' in sexual relations became valued. This new emphasis on honesty and transparency about matters sexual and 'intimate' allowed public revelations about public figures. What could not be said about the private life of President Kennedy (or that of President Roosevelt or Mrs Harold Macmillan) at the beginning of the 1960s had become entirely permissible as public information by the beginning of the 1980s. The rich and the powerful could no longer expect a veil of secrecy to be drawn over their affairs, whether sexual or financial. A culture of revelation had been born, and we

126

continue to live within it. However, the impact of this culture on the lives of all citizens in the West has been complex, in the sense that whilst we now expect to know about the sexual lives of the great, the good and the not-so-good, we remain relatively unsure about what to do with this information. We live in a culture in which it is thought acceptable to ask the present British Prime Minister where he and his wife conceived their fourth child and yet there is less discussion about what we might do with an answer. As consumers of the media it is assumed that we need to know about the 'private' lives of the powerful but the nature of the connections between the private and the public remain unclear. We live in societies which are 'information rich' but arguably 'interpretation poor' – a poverty which results from the collapse or fragmentation of previous moral and social ideas which organized experience and information.

In this world of 'openness' about sexual behaviour it is increasingly taken for granted that there is a single pattern of relations between adult human beings which is desirable. That pattern is no longer one of marriage and heterosexuality but is one of individualized attraction and sexual and emotional fulfilment. Western public life has come (just about) to accept homosexuality and heterosexual cohabitation, but what has become increasingly marginalized is dissent from the dominant expectation of complete personal fulfilment in the private sphere. The inherent individualism of the capitalist ethic has long been noticed by sociologists, but what has generally been refused by the public as a whole has been a consideration of the implications of individualization on relations between the sexes, between partners in love and between children and parents. Weber and Marx both knew and recognized (albeit in different ways) that the impact of the capitalist ethic on the human spirit was considerable: for both men there was an acknowledgement that it was difficult for people of both sexes to live within capitalism without adopting its values. For Marx work within capitalist social relations became 'alienated', for Weber the 'fact of life' within industrial capitalism, with its generalized ethic of rationality and the repression of the erotic, is that we locate within personal relations all the needs that the social world cannot meet. We thus turn to 'love' and to the private for the satisfactions that cannot be ours in other spheres. Unfortunately for many of us, the private sphere is unable to meet the expectations imposed upon it. Hannah Arendt and Philip Aries have described the family as over-loaded or over-burdened with tasks; Christopher Lasch has described the family as 'beseiged'. All these accounts suggest a private space colonized by external expectations.

The contribution of these accounts – and those of Marx and Weber – to love and intimacy in the twenty-first century remain central and persuasive. Marx's particular contribution to the contemporary world remains his fearless recognition of the brutality of capitalist social relations. The actual physical brutality of capitalism may have diminished in the West since the days of *Capital* but what has remained is a relationship between people and capital which is as exploitative in essence as it was in a previous century. Indeed, there is considerable reason to suggest that, far from freeing us from social repression, ideologies of romantic love have made us more, rather than less, vulnerable to the capital market. The fact that we can turn to a sexually liberated sphere of the private world and are free 'to love' as often (and with whom) we choose allows us to construct a personal agenda whose priorities are not those of social engagement. Romance, and romantic love, may have allowed women a greater say in the establishment of heterosexual relationships, but the valorization of romance has often threatened the stability of those relationships.

Whilst Marx defined the terms of engagement of individuals with capitalist production, Weber developed a definitive account of the ethic which makes capitalism possible and long-lasting. In particular, what Weber identified for subsequent generations was 'rationality' – not *the* rational, in the sense of enlightened and critical thought, but the construction of patterns of thought and action designed to serve particular social ends. 'Rationality' marginalizes and renders unacceptable the spontaneous, the apparently 'irrational' and the spiritual. Weber's thesis of the 'iron cage' of bureaucracy is one which remains pertinent to this day: as further aspects of social life are brought within the control and jurisdiction of the state, so it becomes ever more impossible for individuals to achieve a relationship between the social and the personal which allows for the recognition of the emotional. Everyday life and language, which includes expressions about 'letting your hair down' and 'going over the top', suggests that the social world assumes a perilous balance between acceptable, rational, behaviour and the only too easily released behaviour of the irrational, emotional world. We have endlessly ambiguous relationships towards the idea of personal control: on the one hand we identify 'control freaks' but on the other hand praise those who are never 'out of control' and 'know what they are doing'. Western social life makes specific allowance for behaviour which is seen as legitimately different from normal patterns of controlled conduct: at football matches and pop concerts fans are allowed to shout, scream, cry and abuse their fellow human beings in ways which would not be tolerated in other social situations. Equally, occasions such as stag nights derive their interest from the breaking of agreed social boundaries. All these forms of ritualized rule-breaking are socially acceptable (if not universally popular) because of our social sense of the need to 'let off steam' or to indulge in one last fling of irresponsibility before the taking up of adult responsibilities.[5]

There is no evidence to suggest that pop concerts or football matches are becoming any less popular than they once were, but stag nights and other sexual *rites de passage* are increasingly anachronistic as fewer people marry in order to establish sexual relationships or cohabitation. To many people, the transformation of sexual morality since the 1960s would indicate that one aspect of Weber's 'iron cage' has disappeared: people are no longer expected to locate love, and sexuality, exclusively within heterosexual marriage. But to others, the centrality of exclusively individualistic inclinations within marriage, cohabitation and sexual relationships in general has brought not liberation but disappointment and loss. In short, what has occurred is an increasing 'chaos' about love, but not a 'normal chaos' in the sense outlined by the Becks, but a chaos in which individuals are ever more subject to the pressures of the market economy and the demands of a highly individualized and sexualized construction of love.[6] As love becomes more demanding, so fewer individuals can fulfil its expectations and our appetite for love increases. The chaos of love becomes not a creative and engaging chaos between adults, but a chaos of generations whose needs for undemanding and unequivocal love have never been met and who need to turn either to the market place for emotional satisfaction or to that apparently safe haven of the single life.

In the United States and Britain it is now the case that half of all first marriages will end in divorce. Of these marriages not all will have produced children but a considerable proportion will, and numbers of children are now growing up in households which lack one of their biological parents, most commonly their father. A considerable literature now exists which emphasizes the complexity of assessing the impact of divorce on children.[7] Some pundits have a great deal at stake in the issue: to be able to demonstrate children who are clearly damaged by divorce allows those people to point accusing fingers at permissive attitudes to divorce and the irresponsibility of adults. We know, however, that most divorce petitions in England are brought by women against men on the grounds of men's infidelity: the sex most likely to be left literally holding the baby is the sex most anxious to seek disengagement from an unsuccessful relationship. (It may also indicate that it is more often in women's interests than men's to secure financial settlements when marriages break down.) This would suggest that what exists is a different attitude to marriage for women and men: women, despite a recognition that they will be the people responsible for the care of children, are generally not prepared to tolerate or accept male attitudes to marriage which suggest less than exclusivity.

The evidence that we have about the reasons for the breakup of marriage in contemporary Britain can be interpreted in a number of ways. We can read it as an instance of gender differences in views about marriage. We can also read it as an indication of the differences of the sexes towards personal fulfilment and entitlement: men, it would seem from the available material, are more inclined than women to assume that they are entitled to sexual relationships outside marriage. Equally, it would appear that women view the state of marriage as only tolerable if underpinned by male fidelity: better to be alone (with or without children) than with an unfaithful partner. Whatever the reasons, it is apparent that what has disappeared completely is women's fear of being stigmatized or outcast by a failed marriage. The majority of women (like the majority of men) who divorce for the first time subsequently remarry or form other relationships: the desire to be part of a heterosexual couple is obviously still persuasive. Nevertheless, the frequency of rifts between partners demonstrates that there is no longer either a social or a personal barrier to ending an unsatisfactory relationship.

The social consequences of the disappearance or the diminuition of the centrality and prioritization of the state of marriage in the moral discourse of sexuality remain difficult to assess with absolute certainty. We know that today divorce is more frequent and that more children grow up in fractured families. We also know that the consequences (both material and emotional) of divorce for children are worse if contact is lost with one parent and if the material situation of the children and their remaining parent is difficult. It would be absurd to expect anything else: to grow up in poverty and in a one-parent family is evidently less desirable than to grow up in comfortable circumstances with two parents. What is more difficult to assess is the impact that divorce and separation have on the emotional development of children. To assess the differential impact of growing up in a tense and warring household against growing up with a sense of loss and abandonment is extremely difficult and likely to differ according to individual circumstances and personalities. We can now say with certainty that divorce no longer stigmatizes: its very frequency has had a normalizing effect and we have grown to tolerate divorce as much because it is so frequent as because we condone it. One fact which does emerge from the welter of material, opinion and opinionated material about divorce and its impact on children is that the relationship which is most crucial to most children is that with the mother: Britain and the United States are no exception to the global phenomenon of the importance of the tie between mothers and children. Whatever the material or psychic part that fathers play in their children's lives, it is generally mothers with whom children grow up and on whom they depend.[8]

Given the centrality of this tie to the lives of all the world's citizens, it is noticeable how little motherhood and mothering intrudes into male discussion of love and intimacy. For Giddens in *The Transformation of Intimacy* there is an implicit androgyny in his 'democratic' heterosexual lovers: these are not people preoccupied with the demands of children and the household but *individuals* able to live their lives independent of the demands of dependent others. What these individuals have achieved is a state of perfect autonomy: they are the ideal workers for late capitalism and able to conduct their personal lives in the same way as their lives in the workplace: through arrangements of negotiated contract. In the United States the idea of a marriage contract has become part of the new arrangements of marriage: pre-nuptial contracts cover both the organization of property (which is a traditional aspect of marriage contracts) as well as sets of personal expectations and aspirations. Such contracts have yet to become widely significant in Britain but what we can detect in the willingness of individuals both to divorce and to live alone is a refusal of any personal arrangement or relationship which does not meet particular individual requirements and expectations. These expectations arise in part out of the relatively new financial independence of some women – as well as women's increasing sense of the social acceptability of female autonomy – but they also arise, we might conjecture, out of our growing refusal to accept situations and circumstances which do not conform to legalistic and predictable patterns. Arlie Hochschild has pointed out that for some people the world of paid work has become more satisfactory than the world of the household: at work the individual has a given role, can earn respect, has agreed tasks and set hours. Workplaces are nowadays governed by regulations about how individuals can behave: households, so far, are generally not. What Hochschild has also pointed out is that for some women participation in the workplace involves the purchase of the services of other women. Hochschild, in an essay in a collection edited by Will Hutton and Antony Giddens entitled 'Global Care Chains and Emotional Surplus Values,' writes of those 'material expectations' which exploit women of poor countries. The essay makes a very important intervention in suggesting (albeit implicitly) that Giddens's Western world of sexual democracy is possible only through the purchase of domestic assistance to replace the work of Western women and not a renegotiation of the Western domestic contract between women and men.[9]

For many people, women as well as men, it is therefore far more personally rewarding to be in an environment where one's presence is valued and respected and where the terms of engagement are set out. Life in most households does not follow the same predictable pattern of task and reward, time for work and time not to work. On the contrary, life in a household, particularly with small children, involves unbroken hours of work, irregular times for rest and recreation, and few sanctions against unaccept-able behaviour. Even if Arlie Hochschild's world of work presumes interesting, well-paid work in pleasant surround-ings (hardly the norm for many workers), what we can take from her study is the suggestion that many people would like their private world to be organized rather more like their world of paid work – namely, through regulation and contract. It would seem that, even if we do not actually want to be at work for longer hours (or even specifically like or enjoy work), what we do like about paid work is its order, its routine, its relatively structured and organized social relationships and contacts with other adults. For a society which emphasizes the individual, and encourages the idea of individual autonomy, it is paradoxical that apparently many people would actually prefer their emo-tional lives to correspond more closely to generalized rather than individualized patterns of behaviour.

Unfortunately for those many people who might prefer a clearer model for the conduct of personal relations, there are few ways, other than the explicitly authoritarian, in which this can be provided. Patterns of individual be-haviour are often reproduced across generations and it is now the case that both Britain and the Unites States have populations in which the level of divorce continues from one generation to the next – for many people the model of lifelong marriage has not existed for two genera-tions. What has gone with this change has been, as already noted, a change in our attitudes to sexuality. We do not connect sexuality with marriage as we once did, but at the same time we have yet to establish a way of organiz-ing our sexual relations. Michel Foucault established a model for homosexual relationships in his refusal of any regulation other than that of desire: a position as complex in its implications as the arguments about it. If we were to follow Foucault's arguments for heterosexuality we would immediately confront the issues of the construction of heterosexual desire and the terms of heterosexual sexual engagement. Sexual promiscuity in men has long been tolerated in certain quarters under the rubric of 'wild oats' and through the deeply contentious double standard of sexual morality; the extension of the toleration of this behaviour in women has yet to arrive.[10] Nevertheless, it would appear to be the case that for women, rather than for men, there has been little departure from the association of sexual relations with personal affection and commitment, two feelings expressed through the idea which we describe as 'love'.

Thus it is that in the world of the twenty-first century the meaning of love for many people has become far more problematic than it once was, largely because the coercive framework which located sexuality in marriage has disappeared. 'Free' love, the term taken up by its supporters and its opponents in the 1960s, has become love which is often neither 'free' (in the sense of given without ties) nor 'love' (in the sense of the involvement of feelings and emotions other than those of immediate sexual desire). Few people would wish to return to the days before effective contraception, or to those sanctions which separated unmarried women from their children or forced both sexes into unwelcome marriages. There was considerable cruelty and pain in those arrangements about sexuality and sexual relations. Equally, however, there remains cruelty and pain in those sexual relations in which desperate needs for love and affection cannot be met, and in which the parties inflict on each other the losses and absences which they themselves have suffered. In the sphere of love – as in the sphere of paid work or consumption – we have come to expect more, and in expecting more we are perhaps gaining less.

In a conclusion to a discussion about love, therefore, it is important to question the assumption that sexual relations (whether heterosexual or homosexual) are becoming in some way 'better', or, in Giddens's term 'more democratic'. It may be the case that there has been an equalization of expectations between the sexes about sexual engagement and sexual activity, but the assumption that this constitutes democracy in a world in which public social power is so dramatically in the control of men rather than women is rather more problematic. More important still is our assumption that love and sex (and the relation between them) can be separated from other parts of individual lives and the social world in general. We have come to question the distinction between the public and the private worlds, but in many ways still continue to assume that the activities of 'doing love' and 'doing sex' remain inherently part of the private world. That this is not the case has to be the major issue confronting any contemporary discussion of love: the industry of romance has a definition of love which depends upon the fulfilment of the consciously created expectations of the market place. The couple (particularly the heterosexual couple) of late capitalism is a couple who can live, dress, consume and travel in ways which accord with the fantasies of consumption. Appearance, in this world, becomes identity and appearance (in the most general sense of behaviour and personal taste as well as dress) dictates acceptability. When the fictional – but highly recognizable – character Bridget Jones thinks of her new boyfriend, she thinks of him in terms of consumer fantasies:

> Finding it impossible to concentrate on almost anything in the heat except fantasies about going on mini-breaks with Daniel. Head is filled with visions of us lying in glades by rivers, me in long white floaty dress, Daniel and I sitting outside ancient Cornish waterside pub sipping pints in matching striped T-shirts and watching the sun set over the sea; Daniel and I eating candlelit dinners in historic country-house-hotel courtyards.[11]

As readers of her diary will know, Bridget Jones is doomed to disappointment in two ways: the weather on the 'mini-break' is freezing cold and the romantic weather with Daniel turns equally stormy when it is revealed that, unbeknown to Bridget, he has a fiancée.

It would be easy to dismiss Bridget Jones as a silly girl, in a long line of fictional silly girls stretching from Lydia Bennet in Austen's *Pride and Prejudice* to the present day, were it not for the fact that this very silliness has become an increasingly legitimate and accepted part of our culture. When Lydia Bennet could think of nothing except the attractions of the army officers stationed near her home, she is presented by the author as frivolous and thoughtless. Moreover, against Lydia Bennet's behaviour and perception there is set another discourse: that of her father and her elder sisters. Mr Bennet makes no secret of the fact the he regards Lydia as a very silly (and very unappealing) girl. Her sisters, more aware of Lydia's vulnerability than her father, recognize the social consequences of Lydia's silliness. Mr Bennet assumes that no rational or sensible man could be attracted by Lydia, however nubile and however eager to seduce. Jane and Elizabeth Bennet, on the other hand, recognize what Mr Bennet cannot, that Lydia would engage the attentions, not of a sensible man, but of a selfish one. Eventually, it is Jane and Elizabeth who are proved to be the more acute observers of sexual relations: Lydia achieves her goal of marrying George Wickham but only through a forced marriage. As Austen writes in the novel's final pages: 'His [Wickham's] affection of her soon sank into indifference; hers lasted a little longer; and in spite of her youth and her manners she retained all the claims to reputation which her marriage had given her.'[12]

The authorial voice in *Pride and Prejudice* is one which very clearly asserts the desirability of the rational as central in marriage and sexual relations. Sexual attraction (as is made plain in the discussion of numerous achieved marriages in her work) is never in itself a reliable guide to a successful or a happy marriage. What is set out is a model of courtship which is not just 200 chronological years away from the world of Bridget Jones but is qualitatively different in understanding: it is a world in which it is recognized that individuals make marriages and in order to do so there has to be negotiation. That negotiation takes the form of conversation and discussion: its false starts and wrong turnings are those of the achievement of intimacy through fantasy and the sharing of tastes in external objects rather than an understanding of the world. Marianne Dashwood in Austen's *Sense and Sensibility* falls in love with both a handsome physique and a set of shared tastes. Her subsequent illness and heartbreak result from her confusion of taste with understanding.

The tastes which united (or appeared to unite) Marianne Dashwood to Willoughby were, in themselves, literate and educated ones. But they were, Austen had no doubt, external and manufactured objects. The world of *Sense and Sensibility* was historically part of a world which was about to disappear: the explosion of industrial production created the diversity of consumption and possibilities of mobility which are hinted at in Austen's last (unfinished) novel, *Sanditon*. Our world is unlike that of Jane Austen in that it contains endless opportunities for the exercise of personal taste and individual consumption. We have learned, in the 200 years since Austen, a language about ourselves in which we construct ourselves and our relationship to others through our tastes for manufactured objects and situations. Anyone who has read or completed a form for a dating or marriage agency will know that the section on tastes includes questions about inclinations for various forms of consumption. The world of late capitalism is one in which the indicators of personhood are, to a significant extent, created by the market economy.

It is through these images and these choices that we are increasingly inclined to come to know others. A culture in which consumption is paramount is also one in which other choices (for example about politics and religion) may become marginalized or insignificant. The post-Second World War 'peace' of globalization and hegemonic culture has not, as the individual tragedies of the Balkans or Vietnam attest, brought absolute, universal, lasting peace but it has brought the establishment of global markets and the triumph of the market economy as the most ideologically attractive form of social relationship and social organization. Within this context, however, the general social liberalization of the West has been accompanied by ever growing social differences in material affluence: in Britain and the United States there is increasing evidence of increased social inequality and social exclusion.[13] It is in this context – of individual concerns about job security and the costs of healthcare and education – that we love and learn to love. As Oliver James wrote recently:

> Magazines such as *Cosmopolitan* and other media influences too numerous to mention have reinforced the idea that if you are a young woman, the world is your lobster (as Bobby Robson so famously misquoted). . . . In fact, as the popularity of Bridget Jones shows, for many young women the reality has been a nicotine habit and rising levels of anxiety and depression. The great majority end up working in unfulfilling jobs for not much money.[14]

In the same passage, James goes on to argue that late capitalism has created expectations about the good life which it cannot satisfy. For men, just as much as women, the new 'affluence' is also the new squalor, a squalor in which the disruption and interruption of personal lives takes place against the background of material plenty. We are encouraged (in studies such as that by Richard Scase) to suppose that the single life is also the good life, but more sceptically we might consider that the single life is the only *possible* way of life which makes participation in today's workplace feasible. Relations with others demand time and commitment (for intangible rewards) and those relations, in a sexually liberal culture, no longer have any particular or scarcity value. The availability of sex (and its acceptance as an intrinsic part of many social relations, however fleeting) provides little impetus towards the construction and development of long-term relationships. But more than the general impact of sexual liberalization on both sexes we also have to ask if sexual liberalization has been significantly more advantageous for men than for women.

In his essay 'Flirtation' Simmel wrote that women in sexual relations possess the power to be 'the chooser'. But, as he also wrote, 'The power of the woman over consent and refusal is prior to the decision. Once she has decided, in either direction, her power is ended.'[15] This observation – that women's consent to heterosexual relations ends their power over the terms of that engagement – has also been observed, in different ways, by Tolstoy and Freud. It is at the point in *Anna Karenina* where Anna and Vronsky become lovers that the relationship becomes doomed to tragedy: as Freud was to point out in the essay discussed in the previous chapter ('On the Universal Tendency to the Debasement of the Love Object'), it is through the achievement of sexual relations that other forms of perception apart from that of love become apparent. We might argue that all these men were part of a patriarchal culture which equated sexuality with sin (and women with the cause of sin) but equally we could take from their remarks a recognition that sexual desire (for whichever sex by whichever sex) is presented as love but then has either to be translated into an established form of relationship or allowed to exist as such. We are now given the permission to say 'I just want to sleep with you' but the assumptions and constructions surrounding the development of sexual relations into something approaching a lasting relationship have disappeared or been minimized by cultural change. In historical periods in which men were expected to marry (or form social relationships) with the women with whom they had sexual relations there was a space for both the erotic (in that sexuality was repressed and contained) and, through patterns of individualized romance, of the acknowledgement of human diversity and individuality.

This account of the past, and love in the past, is not, it should be emphasized, a statement about some absolute past reality of love and sexuality between the sexes, but a suggestion of the possibilities that need to exist for love to develop. For many writers, in particular Foucault and Ulrich Beck and Elisabeth Beck-Gernsheim, the sexual revolution has allowed us to move to a situation in which it is more, rather than less, likely that love will be possible. Beck and Beck-Gernsheim approvingly quote Foucault's remarks on love:

> Perhaps we are closer now to being witnesses of something beautiful, as Plato recommended, than being the uprooted plastic people we often fear. Perhaps Michel Foucault was right when in 1984, just before his death (having completed his book *The History of Sexuality*), he remarked: 'The idea of morals as something obeying a code of rules is already disappearing. And this lack of any moral code must and will be answered by the search for an aesthetic code of existence.' In place of law, moral precepts, rigidity and a hierarchy of needs Foucault proposed the ancient concept 'the art of life', 'stylizing existence' and 'developing' personal qualities enabling one to make one's own life beautiful.[16]

Since the moment when Foucault wrote his optimistic blueprint for the future, the West has seen the further disappearance of formal legislation about morality and a public increasingly willing to tolerate diverse forms of human sexuality. But the chance to develop the alternative forms of 'guides to life' which Foucault proposed have proved less available for individuals living outside the privilege of Parisian intellectual circles. For the victims, rather than the successful, in late capitalism the resources on hand to develop 'the art of life' are as limited as they ever were, and evidence about the workplace in Britain and the United States suggests that, although the society as a whole may be getting richer (in the sense of its national productivity), significant numbers of individuals are getting poorer and living in conditions of greater material insecurity. The emotional reality of this society is that we are presented with a daily account of the potential ease and luxury of our society (endless technological aids to all kinds of work, easily available credit and widely advertised goods for all tastes and situations) and yet we live in worlds with meagre amounts of paid work, insufficiently funded public institutions and limited free time. A pessimistic reading of this world, in which anyone with access to the internet or an urban environment can immediately access any sexual fantasy they have ever entertained, is that sex is available (and relatively cheap and undemanding) but love is not.

One of the aspects of love which societies prior to ours have recognized is that love demands time and effort. Romance has always been easier to acquire, in that for the past 200 years we have been able either to buy it or to use its manufactured form. But love in any relationship (between adults, friends, parents and children) takes considerably more application. It was not simply because they were more literate and more educated that the better-off could write sagas and poems of courtly and romantic love: they were part of a leisured class which could develop the knowledge of individual difference into idealizations of the other. Our present search for love, which sustains billion dollar industries and institutions of romance, may well become more problematic as our expectations (and sense of entitlement) about the rewards of personal relations increase. But these expectations increase in social worlds which both offer fewer moral and structural guides to personal behaviour and at the same time impose more workplace demands. Enhancing love is not a matter of reintroducing or readopting prohibitions about sexuality or refusing that search for love which has enriched – as well as threatened – the lives of millions of people. It is, however, a matter of recognizing that we do not love, or look for love, in a world of our own. A world of our own may be what we wish to create, but we are doing so in a world in which we can have few resources to love, and to learn to love. The paradox of contemporary love is therefore that in our increasingly bureaucratized Western world we may need to love (and love more) but we have to do this in circumstances which detract from its realization. As

Kathryn Flett, a person who pursued love with twentieth-century dedication, has written:

> How does one learn about love? All through my childhood, I knew about my parents' childhoods. I knew what unhappiness was because they told me about it. . . . Children ultimately, ideally, need to be able to grow up and become adults who choose to do the leaving, rather than have their parents leave them, either physically or psychologically, while they are still children. Because if that happens, they often keep searching desperately for 'love', when all they are really looking for is some place they can feel safe.[17]

This comment suggests much of the heartbreak that is part of the contemporary search for love. We have not, in the West, outlawed sexual desire in the way which George Orwell predicted in *1984*, but we have, arguably, de-eroticized sexuality to such an extent that we achieve the personally brutal relationships which *1984* suggested. In this context, it may seem contradictory to propose that we abandon the idea of love. Love, it might appear, is what we need to enlarge and expand. But the proposal is not that we abandon love in the sense of care and commitment, but we abandon it in its romanticized and commercialized form. Love is a four letter word and the care (and prohibition) once evident about the use of other four letter words might well be reasserted in the case of love. The proposal, therefore, is that just as love was part of a process of modernization, so our understanding of love demands – and deserves – retrieval from those careless and irrational spheres to which it has been assigned. At the conclusion to Mozart's opera *Così fan tutte* the central characters (all made to look ridiculous by their romantic fantasies) join in a hymn to rational love and understanding.[18] Rather than regarding the rational as the cold and uncaring enemy of love, we might well regard it as its only true defender in a social world awash with deadly cocktails of romance, hedonism and personal entitlement.

Notes

Chapter 1   What is this Thing Called Love?

1   See, amongst other histories of love, Irving Singer, *The Nature of Love* (University of Chicago Press, Chicago, 1984); V. J. Seidler, *The Moral Limits of Modernity: Love and Inequality* (Macmillan, London, 1990) and Denis de Rougemont, *Love in the Western World* (Pantheon, New York, 1956); Catherine Belsey, *Desire: Love Stories in Western Culture* (Blackwell Publishers, Oxford, 1994).

2   John Donne, 'The good morrow', from *John Donne, Poetical Works* (Oxford University Press, Oxford, 1977), p. 7.

3   Anthony Giddens, *The Transformation of Intimacy* (Polity, Cambridge, 1992); Ulrich Beck and Elisabeth Beck-Gernsheim, *The Normal Chaos of Love* (Polity, Cambridge, 1995); Wendy Langford, *Revolutions of the Heart: Power and the Delusions of Love* (Routledge, London, 1999).

4   Giddens, *The Transformation of Intimacy*, p. 58.

5   Jeffrey Weeks has argued this case: see Jeffrey Weeks, *Invented Moralities: Sexual Values in an Age of Uncertainty* (Polity, Cambridge, 1995).

6   Stevi Jackson, 'Even Sociologists Fall in Love: An Exploration in the Sociology of Emotions', *Sociology*, 27, 2 (1993), pp. 201–20.

7   Max Weber, 'Religious Rejections of the World and their Directions', in H. Gerth and C. W. Mills (eds), *From Max*

Weber (Routledge, London, 1948), pp. 343–50; Georg Simmel, 'On Love', in *Georg Simmel: On Women, Sexuality and Love*, ed. Guy Oakes (Yale University Press, London, 1984), pp. 153–92; Talcott Parsons, 'Democracy and Social Structure in pre-Nazi Germany', in *Essays in Sociological Theory*, ed. Talcott Parsons (Free Press, New York, 1964), pp. 104–23; Jürgen Habermas, *The Philosophical Discourse of Modernity* (MIT Press, Cambridge, Mass., 1990).

8 Niklas Luhmann, *Love as Passion: The Codification of Intimacy* (Harvard University Press, Cambridge, Mass., 1986).

9 Judith Brown, *Immodest Acts: The Life of a Lesbian Nun in Renaissance Italy* (Oxford University Press, Oxford, 1986).

10 See the account of the pressures on Prince Charles to marry in Jonathan Dimbleby, *The Prince of Wales: A Biography* (Warner Books, London, 1995), pp. 338–42.

11 Ibid., p. 24.

12 Ibid., pp. 49–92 and Sarah Bradford, *Elizabeth* (Mandarin, London, 1997), pp. 277–83.

13 The reasons for marriage as given in the Book of Common Prayer are 'the procreation of children; a remedy against sin and to avoid fornication' and (lastly) the 'mutual society, help, and comfort' of husband and wife.

14 Julie Burchill, *Diana* (Orion, London, 1999) and Beatrix Campbell, *Diana, Princess of Wales: How Sexual Politics Shook the Monarchy* (Women's Press, London, 1998).

15 Elizabeth Wilson, 'The Unbearable Lightness of Diana', *New Left Review*, November/December 1997, pp. 136–45; Joan Smith, 'Diana: une femme du passé', *Le Monde Diplomatique*, October 1997, p. 32.

16 Jeffrey Weeks, 'Private Pleasures and Public Policy', in *Sexuality* ed. Jeffrey Weeks (Tavistock, London, 1986), pp. 110–20.

17 See John Jervis, *Transgressing the Modern* (Blackwell Publishers, Oxford, 1999), chs 1 and 2.

18 See the discussion in Judith Butler, *Gender Trouble* (Routledge, London, 1990).

19 Erving Goffmann, *Asylums* (Penguin, Harmondsworth, 1968).

20 Harold Garfinkel, *Studies in Ethno Methodology* (Prentice-Hall, Englewood Cliffs, NJ, 1967), pp. 116–85.

21 Marjorie Garber, *Cross Dressing* (Penguin, London, 1993).
22 For example, to appear as 'a gentleman' involved the responsibility for behaving as such. See A. Bryson, 'The Rhetoric
of Status: Gesture, Demeanour and the Image of the Gentleman in 16th and 17th Century England', in L. Gent and
N. Llewellyn (eds), *Renaissance Bodies* (Reaktion Books,
London, 1990), p. 149.
23 See the considerable literature on the stressful, long hours
culture of the workplace, for example, Patricia Hewitt,
About Time: The Revolution in Work and Family Life
(Rivers Oram Press, London, 1993).
24 Gillian Rose, *Love's Work* (Chatto and Windus, London,
1995), p. 127.
25 See Louie Burghes, 'Debates on Disruption' in Elizabeth
Bortolaia Silva (ed.), *Good Enough Mothering?* (Routledge,
London, 1996), pp. 157–74.
26 Michele Barrett and Mary McIntosh, *The Anti-Social Family*
(Verso, London, 1982).

Chapter 2　Going Back

1 See the review of material on the family in Jane Lewis (with
Jessica Datta and Sophie Sarre), *Individualism and Commitment in Marriage and Cohabitation* (London, Lord
Chancellor's Department, Research Series 8/99, September
1999.
2 See Liz Stanley, ' "From self-made women" to "women's
made-selves"?', in Tess Cosslett, Celia Lury and Penny
Summerfield (eds), *Feminism and Autobiography* (Routledge, London, 2000), pp. 40–60.
3 Max Weber, 'Bureaucracy', in H. Gerth and C. W. Mills
(eds), *From Max Weber* (Routledge, London, 1970),
pp. 196–244.
4 Percy Shelley, quoted in Miranda Seymour, *Mary Shelley*
(John Murray, London, 2000), p. 96.
5 Tony Tanner, *Adultery and the Novel* (Johns Hopkins
University Press, London, 1979), p. 15.
6 Jane Austen, *Pride and Prejudice* (Penguin, Harmondsworth,
1965), p. 228.
7 Ibid., p. 231.

8   See the lives of Jane Austen by Claire Tomalin, *Jane Austen: A Life* (Penguin, London, 1998) and David Nokes, *Jane Austen* (Fourth Estate, London, 1998).

9   Alasdair Macintyre, *After Virtue* (Duckworth, London, 1985), pp. 181–7.

10 Michel Foucault, *The History of Sexuality*, vol. 1 (Allen Lane, London, 1979).

11 An interesting discussion of these issues is Anne Phillips, 'Pluralism, Solidarity and Change', in Jeffrey Weeks (ed.), *The Lesser Evil and the Greater Good* (Rivers Oram Press, London, 1994), pp. 235–52.

12 See M. Evans, *Jane Austen and the State* (Tavistock, London, 1987) and Roger Sales, *Jane Austen and Representations of Regency England* (Routledge, London, 1996).

13 Juliet Barker, *The Brontës* (Orion, London, 1997), p. 547.

14 Susan Meyer, *Imperialism at Home: Race and Victorian Women's Fiction* (Cornell University Press, Ithaca, NY, 1996), pp. 60–95.

15 The idea of the 'invention' of tradition has been explored in E. J. Hobsbawm and Terence Ranger (eds), *The Invention of Tradition* (Cambridge University Press, Cambridge, 1997).

16 Kathryn Flett, *The Heart Shaped Bullet* (Picador, London, 1999).

17 Ibid., p. 48.

18 Ibid., p. 49.

19 Ibid., p. 53.

20 Ibid., p. 23.

21 Sylvia Plath, *The Bell Jar* (Faber and Faber, London, 1963).

22 H. G. Wells, *Ann Veronica* (first published in 1909; Dent, London, 1993); Arnold Bennett, *Anna of the Five Towns* (first published in 1902; Penguin, London, 1999); D. H. Lawrence, *Women in Love* (first published in 1920; Penguin, London, 1995); Sinclair Lewis, *Babbitt* (Signet, New York, 1961); and George Orwell, *Coming Up for Air* (Penguin, Harmondsworth, 1963).

23 John Osborne, *Look Back in Anger* (first performed in 1956).

24 George Orwell, *1984* (Penguin, Harmondsworth, 1962).

25 Michael Shelden, *George Orwell* (Harcourt, Brace, Jovanovich, New York, 1991), p. 323.

26 Sheila Jeffreys, *Anticlimax* (Women's Press, London, 1990), pp. 91–135.

27 Richard Hoggart, *The Uses of Literacy* (Penguin, Harmondsworth, 1962), p. 206.

28 John Jervis, *Exploring the Modern* (Blackwell Publishers, Oxford, 1998), chs 4 and 5.

29 Ross McKibbin, *Classes and Cultures: England 1918–1951* (Oxford University Press, Oxford, 1998), pp. 327–8.

30 R. and K. Titmuss, *Parents Revolt: A Study of the Declining Birthrate in Acquisitive Societies* (Secker and Warburg, London, 1942).

31 A. J. P. Taylor, *English History 1914–1945* (Oxford University Press, Oxford, 1965), p. 302.

32 Christopher Lasch, *Haven in a Heartless World* (Norton, New York, 1995).

33 Arlie Hochschild, *The Time Bind: When Work Becomes Home and Home Becomes Work* (Metropolitan Books and Henry Holt and Co., New York, 1997).

34 Giddens, *The Transformation of Intimacy*.

35 Ibid., p. 188.

36 The gender politics of reason have been discussed by Rose Coser in 'The Principle of Patriarchy: The Case of the Magic Flute', *Signs*, 4, 2 (1978), pp. 337–49.

37 Ros Coward, *Sacred Cows: Is Feminism up to the Nineties?* (HarperCollins, London, 1998); Susan Faludi, *Stuffed: The Betrayal of Modern Man* (Chatto and Windus, London, 1999).

38 For studies of 'time poverty' individual and social attitudes to the use of time see 'Culture at Work' by John Eldridge in Huw Beynon and Pandeli Glavanis (eds), *Patterns of Social Inequality* (Longman, London, 1999), pp. 97–109.

Chapter 3 The Language of Love

1 Richard Hoggart, *An Imagined Life: Life and Times, 1959–1961* (Chatto and Windus, London, 1992), p. 57.

2 Ibid., p. 52.

3 There is now a considerable specialization within 'dating' and 'introduction' agencies. For example, an organization

called 'Drawing Down the Moon' caters for 'young professionals with a creative bent' (to use their self-description)
to 'Natural Friends', which offers its services to 'non-
materialistic non-smokers who like the outdoors and are
interested in animal welfare'.

4   See Penrose Halson, *Happily Ever After: How to Meet your
    Match* (Pan, London, 2000).
5   *Independent on Sunday*, 21 November 1999.
6   This was awarded by the British Board of Film Censors
    in 1999. There is a discussion of the work of the director
    Lars von Trier by John Roberts in *New Left Review*, 238
    (November/December 1999), pp. 141–9.
7   Jeffreys, *Anticlimax*.
8   Barbara Ehrenreich, *The Hearts of Men: American Dreams
    and the Flight from Commitment* (Pluto, London, 1983).
9   Germaine Greer, *The Whole Woman* (Transworld, London,
    1999).
10 Ibid., pp. 181–91.
11 Kathleen Barry, *The Prostitution of Sexuality: The Global
    Exploitation of Women* (New York University Press, Lon-
    don, 1995).
12 The links between the economic and the moral 'Right'
    are discussed in Rebecca Klatch, *Women of the New Right*
    (Temple University Press, Philadelphia, 1987).
13 George Ritzer, *The McDonaldization Thesis* (Sage, London,
    1998).
14 Ehrenreich, *The Hearts of Men*, pp. 42–51.
15 Barry, *The Prostitution of Sexuality*.
16 Edward Said, *Culture and Imperialism* (Vintage, London,
    1994).
17 Andrew Motion, *Philip Larkin: A Writer's Life* (Faber and
    Faber, London, 1994).
18 Helen Fielding, *Bridget Jones's Diary* (Picador, London,
    1998), p. 13.
19 Flett, *The Heart Shaped Bullet*, p. 55.
20 Deborah Philips, 'Shopping for Men: The Single Woman
    Narrative', *Women: A Cultural Review*, 11, 3 (2000),
    pp. 238–51.
21 Ibid., p. 242.
22 Jane Austen, *Sense and Sensibility* (Penguin, Harmondsworth,
    1971), p. 122.

23 Richard Hoggart, *A Local Habitation: Life and Times, 1918–1940* (Chatto and Windus, London, 1988), p. 58.

24 Richard Hoggart, *A Sort of Clowning: Life and Times, 1940–1959* (Chatto and Windus, London, 1990), p. 27.

25 Norbert Elias, *The Civilizing Process*, vol. 1: *The History of Manners* (Basil Blackwell, Oxford, 1978).

26 Philip Larkin, *Collected Poems* (Faber and Faber, London, 1988), p. 167.

27 Shere Hite, *Women and Love: A Cultural Revolution in Progress* (Penguin, London, 1987).

28 Tanner, *Adultery and the Novel*, p. 52.

Chapter 4   The Rules of Love

1 Friedrich Engels, *The Origin of the Family, Private Property and the State* (Penguin, Harmondsworth, 1985), p. 102; Simone de Beauvoir, *The Prime of Life* (Penguin, Harmondsworth, 1965), p. 75.

2 Catharine MacKinnon, *Towards a Feminist Theory of the State* (Harvard Univeristy Press, Cambridge, Mass., 1989).

3 Alan Sillitoe, *Saturday Night and Sunday Morning* (Grafton, London, 1958) and Stan Barstow, *A Kind of Loving* (Penguin, Harmondsworth, 1960).

4 Barstow, *A Kind of Loving*, p. 249.

5 Carol Gilligan, *In a Different Voice. Psychological Theory and Women's Development* (Harvard University Press, Cambridge, Mass., 1982).

6 See Nancy Fraser, *Justice Interruptus: Critical Reflections on the 'Post-socialist' Condition* (Routledge, London, 1997).

7 L. M. Brown and Carol Gilligan, *Meeting at the Crossroads: Women's Psychology and Girls' Development* (Harvard University Press, Cambridge, Mass., 1992).

8 Mary Hamer, 'Listen to the Voice: An Interview with Carol Gilligan', *Women: A Cultural Review*, 10, 2 (1999), p. 178.

9 Ibid., p. 178.

10 Ellie Lee (ed.) *Abortion Law and Politics Today* (Macmillan, London, 1998).

11 For a critical evaluation of Gilligan's work see Janet Sayers, *Sexual Contradictions* (Tavistock, London, 1986), pp. 18–20, 70–73.

12 Judith Warkowitz, *Prostitution and Victorian Society: Women, Class and the State* (Cambridge University Press, Cambridge, 1982).

13 Barstow, *A Kind of Loving*, p. 197.

14 Ibid., p. 272.

15 On the relationship between sexuality, culture and economy see Harriet Bradley and Steve Fenton, 'Reconciling Culture and Economy: Ways Forward in the Analysis of Ethnicity and Gender', in Larry Ray and Andrew Sayer (eds), *Culture and Economy after the Cultural Turn* (Sage, London, 1999), pp. 112–34.

16 Alan Clark, *Diaries* (Weidenfeld and Nicolson, London, 1993), p. 67.

17 Catherine Hakim, 'Diversity and Choice in the Sexual Contract', in G. Dench (ed.), *Rewriting the Sexual Contract* (Institute of Community Studies, London, 1997), pp. 165–79.

18 *Guardian*, 22 November 1999, p. 4.

19 Mary Douglas, *Purity and Danger* (Pelican, Harmondsworth, 1970).

20 *Guardian*, 22 November 1999, p. 4.

21 On the diverse cultures of homosexuality see Jeffrey Weeks and Janet Holland (eds), *Sexual Cultures: Communities, Values and Intimacy* (Macmillan, London, 1996).

22 Mary Shelley, *Frankenstein* (Oxford University Press, Oxford, 1993), p. 37.

23 Francesca Cancian, *Love in America: Gender and Self-Development* (Cambridge University Press, Cambridge, 1987); Elaine Tyler May, *Great Expectations: Marriage and Divorce in Post-Victorian America* (University of Chicago Press, Chicago, 1980).

24 There is an extensive literature on this subject: see Bren Neale, *Negotiating Parenthood: A Framework for Research* (Gender Analysis and Policy Unit, Leeds, 1995), pp. 1–31 for a full bibliography.

25 See Jervis, *Transgressing the Modern*, ch. 6.

Chapter 5 The Limits of Love

1 Marie Stopes, *Married Love* (Putnam, London, 1923).

2 Naomi Klein, *No Logo* (Flamingo, London, 2000); Richard Sennett, *Corrosion of Character* (Norton, New York, 1998).

3   David Frisby, *Fragments of Modernity* (Polity Cambridge, 1985).
4   Sigmund Freud, 'On the Universal Tendency to Debasement in the Sphere of Love', in *The Pelican Freud Library*, ed. James Strachey, vol. 7 (Penguin, Harmondsworth, 1962), pp. 247–64.
5   Ibid., p. 251.
6   Ibid., p. 256.
7   Ibid., p. 254.
8   Rosemary Crompton, *Women and Work in Contemporary Britain* (Blackwell Publishers, Oxford, 1997).
9   Tony Parsons, *Man and Boy* (HarperCollins, London, 2000).
10 Elisabeth Beck-Gernsheim, 'On the Way to a Post-Familial Family', in Mike Featherstone (ed.), *Love and Eroticism* (Sage, London, 1999), p. 65.
11 Sam Whimster with Gottfried Hener, 'Otto Gross and Else Jaffé and Max Weber', in Featherstone, *Love and Eroticism*, p. 147.
12 Elizabeth Wilson, 'Bohemian Love', *Theory, Culture and Society*, 15, 3–4 (1999), pp. 111–27.
13 Helen Fielding, *The Edge of Reason* (Picador, London, 2000), p. 94.
14 Annette Lawson, *Adultery* (Oxford University Press, Oxford, 1988), pp. 77–88.
15 Ibid., p. 209.
16 Ibid., p. 17.
17 John Updike, *Couples* (André Deutsch, London, 1968), p. 458.
18 Martin Amis, *Experience* (Vintage, London, 2001), p. 99.
19 Amy Levy, 'Ballad of Religion and Marriage', *Persephone Quarterly*, 9 (2001), p. 2.
20 David Lodge, *How Far Can You Go?* (Penguin, Harmondsworth, 1980), p. 153.
21 Philip Larkin, *Collected Poems* (Faber and Faber, London, 1988), p. 111.
22 Ibid., p. 214.
23 Robert Putnam, 'Bowling Alone: America's Declining Social Capital', *Journal of Democracy*, 6, 1 (January 1995), pp. 71–8.
24 Hannah Arendt, *The Human Condition* (Doubleday, New York, 1959).

25 Krishan Kumar, 'Home: The Promise and Predicament of Private Life at the End of the Twentieth Century', in J. Wentraub and K. Kumar (eds), *Public and Private in Thought and Practice: Perspectives on a Grand Dichotomy* (University of Chicago Press, Chicago, 1997).

Chapter 6   The Future of Love

1 Langford, *Revolutions of the Heart*.
2 Ibid., pp. 1–22.
3 Ibid., p. 21.
4 Ibid., p. 151.
5 R. Shields, 'The "System of Pleasure": Liminality and the Carnivalesque at Brighton', *Theory, Culture and Society*, 7, 1 (1990).
6 See Bryan Turner, 'The Sociology and Anthropology of the Family', in Bryan Turner (ed.), *Classical Sociology* (Sage, London, 1999). pp. 232–45.
7 But it is also important to note, as Lawrence Stone has pointed out, that the present impact of divorce on children is not unlike that of death (of parents) in the nineteenth century. See Lawrence Stone, *The Family, Sex and Marriage in England, 1500–1800* (Harper and Row, New York, 1977), pp. 58–64. Also on the variance in the idea of 'the family' see John Gillis, *A World of their Own Making* (Oxford University Press, Oxford, 1997), pp. 3–19.
8 The psychological and social consequences of this relationship were forcefully discussed by Nancy Chodorow in *The Reproduction of Mothering* (University of California Press, London, 1987).
9 A. Hochschild, *The Time Bind*, and 'Global Care Chains and Emotional Surplus Value', in Will Hutton and Anthony Giddens (eds), *On the Edge: Living with Global Capitalism* (Cape, London, 2000), pp. 130–46.
10 Lesley Holly (ed.), *Girls and Sexuality* (Open University Press, Milton Keynes, 1987).
11 Fielding, *Bridget Jones's Diary*, p. 141.
12 Austen, *Pride and Prejudice*, p. 394.
13 Larry Elliott and Dan Atkinson, *The Age of Insecurity* (Verso, London, 1998) and N. Davies, *Dark Heart: The*

Shocking Truth about Hidden Britain (Chatto and Windus, London, 1997).

14 Oliver James, *Guardian*, January 2000.
15 Georg Simmel, 'Flirtation', in *George Simmel: On Women, Sexuality and Love*, ed. G. Oakes.
16 Beck and Beck-Gernsheim, *The Normal Chaos of Love*, p. 183.
17 Flett, *The Heart Shaped Bullet*, p. 220.
18 'Fortunate is the man who takes / everything for the best, / and in all events and trials / allows himself to be led by reason' / (*Così fan tutte*, Finale, Act II).

Bibliography

Books

Amis, K. 1954: *Lucky Jim*. London: Gollancz.

Amis, M. 2001: *Experience*. London: Vintage.

Arendt, H. 1959: *The Human Condition*. New York: Doubleday.

Austen, J. 1965: *Pride and Prejudice*. Harmondsworth: Penguin.

Austen, J. 1971: *Sense and Sensibility*. Harmondsworth: Penguin.

Barker, J. 1997: *The Brontës*. London: Orion.

Barrett, M. and McIntosh, M. 1982: *The Anti-Social Family*. London: Verso.

Barry, K. 1995: *The Prostitution of Sexuality: The Global Exploitation of Women*. London: New York University Press.

Barstow, S. 1960: *A Kind of Loving*. Harmondsworth: Penguin.

Beck, U. and Beck-Gernsheim, E. 1995: *The Normal Chaos of Love*. Cambridge: Polity.

Belsey, C. 1994: *Desire: Love Stories in Western Culture*. Oxford: Blackwell Publishers.

Bennett, A. 1999: *Anna of the Five Towns*. London: Penguin.

Beynon, H. and Glavanis, P. (eds) 1999: *Patterns of Social Inequality*, London: Longman.

Bradford, S. 1997: *Elizabeth*. London: Mandarin.

Brown, L. M. and Gilligan, C. 1992: *Meeting at the Crossroads: Women's Psychology and Girls' Development*. Cambridge, Mass.: Harvard University Press.

Burchill, J. 1999: *Diana*. London: Orion.

155

Bibliography

Butler, J. 1990: *Gender Trouble*. London: Routledge.

Campbell, B. 1998: *Diana, Princess of Wales: How Sexual Politics Shook the Monarchy*. London: Women's Press.

Cancian, F. 1987: *Love in America: Gender and Self-Development*. Cambridge: Cambridge University Press.

Chodorow, N. 1987: *The Reproduction of Mothering*. London: University of California Press.

Clark, A. 1993: *Diaries*. London: Weidenfeld and Nicolson.

Cosslett, T., Lury, C. and Summerfield, P. (eds) 2000: *Feminism and Autobiography*. London: Routledge.

Coward, R. 1984: *Female Desire: Women's Sexuality Today*. London: Paladin.

Coward, R. 1998: *Sacred Cows: Is Feminism up to the Nineties?* London: HarperCollins.

Crompton, R. 1997: *Women and Work in Contemporary Britain*. Oxford: Blackwell Publishers.

Davies, N. 1997: *Dark Heart: The Shocking Truth about Hidden Britain*. London: Chatto and Windus.

de Beauvoir, S. 1965: *The Prime of Life*. Harmondsworth: Penguin.

Dench, G. (ed.) 1997: *Rewriting the Sexual Contract*. London: Institute of Community Studies.

de Rougemont, D. 1956: *Love in the Western World*. New York: Pantheon.

Dimbleby, J. 1995: *The Prince of Wales: A Biography*. London: Warner Books.

Donne, J. 1977: *John Donne, Poetical Works*. Oxford: Oxford University Press.

Douglas, M. 1970: *Purity and Danger*. Harmondsworth: Pelican.

Ehrenreich, B. 1983: *The Hearts of Men: American Dreams and the Flight from Commitment*. London: Pluto.

Elias, N. 1978: *The Civilizing Process*, vol. 1: *The History of Manners*. Oxford: Basil Blackwell.

Elliott, L. and Atkinson, D. 1998: *The Age of Insecurity*. London: Verso.

Engels, F. 1985: *The Origin of the Family, Private Property and the State*. Harmondsworth: Penguin.

Evans, M. (1987): *Jane Austen and the State*. London: Tavistock.

Faludi, S. 1999: *Stuffed: The Betrayal of Modern Man*. London: Chatto and Windus.

Featherstone, M. (ed.) (1999) *Love and Eroticism*. London: Sage.

Bibliography

Fielding, H. 1998: *Bridget Jones's Diary*. London: Picador.

Fielding, H. 2000: *The Edge of Reason*. London: Picador.

Flett, K. 1999: *The Heart Shaped Bullet*. London: Picador.

Foucault, M. 1979: *The History of Sexuality*, vol. 1. London: Allen Lane.

Fraser, N. 1997: *Justice Interruptus: Critical Reflections on the 'Post-socialist' Condition*. London: Routledge.

Freud, S. 1986: *The Pelican Freud Library*, ed. J. Strachey, vol. 7. Harmondsworth: Penguin.

Frisby, D. 1985: *Fragments of Modernity*. Cambridge: Polity.

Garber, M. 1993: *Cross Dressing*. London: Penguin.

Garfinkel, H. 1967: *Studies in Ethno Methodology*. Englewood Cliffs, NJ: Prentice-Hall.

Gent, L. and Llewellyn, N. (eds) 1990: *Renaissance Bodies*. London: Reaktion Books.

Gerth, H. and Mills, C. W. (eds) 1994: *From Max Weber*. London: Routledge.

Giddens, A. 1992: *The Transformation of Intimacy*. Cambridge: Polity.

Gilligan, C. 1982: *In a Different Voice: Psychological Theory and Women's Development*. Cambridge, Mass.: Harvard University Press.

Gillis, J. 1997: *A World of their Own Making*. Oxford: Oxford University Press.

Goffmann, E. 1968: *Asylums*. Harmondsworth: Penguin.

Greer, G. 1999: *The Whole Woman*. London: Transworld.

Habermas, J. 1990: *The Philosophical Discourse of Modernity*. Cambridge, Mass.: MIT Press.

Halson, P. 2000: *Happily Ever After: How to Meet your Match*. London: Pan.

Hewitt, P. 1993: *About Time: The Revolution in Work and Family Life*. London: Rivers Oram Press.

Hite, S. 1987: *Women and Love: A Cultural Revolution in Progress*. London: Penguin.

Hobsbawm, E. J. and Ranger. T. (eds) 1997: *The Invention of Tradition*. Cambridge: Cambridge University Press.

Hochschild, A. 1997: *The Time Bind: When Work Becomes Home and Home Becomes Work*. New York: Metropolitan Books and Henry Holt and Co.

Hoggart, R. 1962: *The Uses of Literacy*. Harmondsworth: Penguin.

157

Bibliography

Hoggart, R. 1988: *A Local Habitation: Life and Times, 1918–1940*. London: Chatto and Windus.

Hoggart, R. 1990: *A Sort of Clowning: Life and Times, 1940–1959*. London: Chatto and Windus.

Hoggart, R. 1992: *An Imagined Life: Life and Times, 1959–1961*. London: Chatto and Windus.

Holly, L. (ed.) 1987: *Girls and Sexuality*. Milton Keynes: Open University Press.

Hutton, W. and Giddens, A. (eds) 2000: *On the Edge: Living with Global Capitalism*. London: Cape.

Jeffreys, S. 1990: *Anticlimax*. London: Women's Press.

Jervis, J. 1998: *Exploring the Modern*. Oxford: Blackwell Publishers.

Jervis, J. 1999: *Transgressing the Modern*. Oxford: Blackwell Publishers.

Klatch, R. 1987: *Women of the New Right*. Philadelphia: Temple University Press.

Klein, N. 2000: *No Logo*. London: Flamingo.

Langford, W. 1999: *Revolutions of the Heart: Gender, Power and the Delusions of Love*. London: Routledge.

Larkin, P. 1988: *Collected Poems*. London: Faber and Faber.

Lasch, C. 1995: *Haven in a Heartless World*. New York: Norton.

Lawrence, D. H. 1995: *Women in Love*. London: Penguin.

Lawson, A. 1988: *Adultery*. Oxford: Oxford University Press.

Lee, E. (ed.) 1998: *Abortion Law and Politics Today*. London: Macmillan.

Lewis, J. (with Jessica Datta and Sophie Sarre) (1999): *Individualism and Commitment in Marriage and Cohabitation*. London: Lord Chancellor's Department, Research Series 8/99.

Lewis, S. 1961: *Babbit*. New York: Signet.

Lodge, D. 1980: *How Far Can You Go?* Harmondsworth: Penguin.

Luhmann, N. 1986: *Love as Passion: The Codification of Intimacy*. Cambridge, Mass.: Harvard University Press.

Macintyre, A. 1985: *After Virtue*. London: Duckworth.

McKibbin, R. 1998: *Classes and Cultures: England 1918–1951*. Oxford: Oxford University Press.

MacKinnon, C. 1989: *Towards a Feminist Theory of the State*. Cambridge, Mass.: Harvard Univeristy Press.

Meyer, S. 1996: *Imperialism at Home: Race and Victorian Women's Fiction*. Ithaca, NY: Cornell University Press.

Motion, A. 1994: *Philip Larkin: A Writer's Life*. London: Faber and Faber.

Neale, B. 1995: *Negotiating Parenthood: A Framework for Research*. Leeds: Gender Analysis and Policy Unit.

Nokes, D. 1998: *Jane Austen*. London: Fourth Estate.

Orwell, G. 1962: *1984*. Harmondsworth: Penguin.

Orwell, G. 1963: *Coming Up for Air*. Harmondsworth: Penguin.

Parsons, T. (ed.) 1964: *Essays in Sociological Theory*. New York: Free Press.

Parsons, T. 2000: *Man and Boy*. London: HarperCollins.

Pearce, L. and Strachey, J. (eds) 1995: *Romance Revisited*. London: Lawrence and Wishart.

Plath, S. (1963): *The Bell Jar*. London: Faber and Faber.

Ray, L. and Sayer, A. (eds) 1999: *Culture and Economy after the Cultural Turn*. London: Sage.

Ritzer, G. 1998: *The McDonaldization Thesis*. London: Sage.

Rose, G. 1995: *Love's Work*. London: Chatto and Windus.

Said, E. 1994: *Culture and Imperialism*. London: Vintage.

Sales, R. 1996: *Jane Austen and Representations of Regency England*. London: Routledge.

Sayers, J. 1986: *Sexual Contradictions*. London: Tavistock.

Seidler, V. J. 1990: *The Moral Limits of Modernity: Love and Inequality*. London: Macmillan.

Sennett, R. 1998: *Corrosion of Character*. New York: Norton.

Seymour, M. 2000: *Mary Shelley*, London: John Murray.

Shelden, M. 1991: *George Orwell*. New York: Harcourt, Brace, Jovanovich.

Shelley, M. 1993: *Frankenstein*. Oxford: Oxford University Press.

Sillitoe, A. 1985: *Saturday Night and Sunday Morning*. London: Grafton.

Silva, E. B. (ed.) 1996: *Good Enough Mothering?* London: Routledge.

Simmel, G. 1984: *Georg Simmel: On Women, Sexuality and Love*, ed. G. Oakes. London: Yale University Press.

Singer, I. 1984: *The Nature of Love*. Chicago: University of Chicago Press.

Stone, L. 1977: *The Family, Sex and Marriage in England, 1500–1800*. New York: Harper and Row.

Stopes, M. 1923: *Married Love*. London: Putnam.

Tanner, T. 1990: *Adultery and the Novel*. London: Johns Hopkins University Press.

159

Bibliography

Taylor, A. J. P. 1965: *English History 1914–1945*. Oxford: Oxford University Press.

Titmuss, R. and Titmuss, K. 1942: *Parents Revolt: A Study of the Declining Birthrate in Acquisitive Societies*. London: Secker and Warburg.

Tomalin, C. 1998: *Jane Austen: A Life*. London: Penguin.

Turner, B. 1992: *Regulating Bodies*. London: Routledge.

Turner, B. (ed.) 1999: *Classical Sociology*. London: Sage.

Tyler May, E. 1980: *Great Expectations: Marriage and Divorce in Post-Victorian America*. Chicago: University of Chicago Press.

Updike, J. 1968: *Couples*. London: André Deutsch.

Warkowitz, J. 1982: *Prostitution and Victorian Society: Women, Class and the State*. Cambridge: Cambridge University Press.

Weeks, J. (ed.) 1986: *Sexuality*. London: Tavistock.

Weeks, J. (ed.) 1994: *The Lesser Evil and the Greater Good*. London: Rivers Oram Press.

Weeks, J. 1995: *Invented Moralities: Sexual Values in an Age of Uncertainty*. Cambridge: Polity.

Weeks, J. and Holland, J. (eds) 1996: *Sexual Cultures: Communities, Values and Intimacy*. London: Macmillan.

Wells, H. G. 1993: *Ann Veronica*. London: Dent.

Wentraub, J. and Kumar, K. (eds) 1997: *Public and Private in Thought and Practice: Perspectives on a Grand Dichotomy*. Chicago: University of Chicago Press.

Journals

Coser, R. 1978: 'The Principle of Patriarchy: The Case of the Magic Flute'. *Signs*, 4 (2), 337–49.

Hamer, M. 1999: 'Listen to the Voice: An Interview with Carol Gilligan.' *Women: A Cultural Review*, 10 (2), 173.

Jackson, S. 1993: 'Even Sociologists Fall in Love: An Exploration in the Sociology of Emotions'. *Sociology*, 27 (2), 201–20.

Levy, A. 2001: 'Ballad of Religion and Marriage'. *Persephone Quarterly*, 9 (Spring), 2.

Philips, D. 2000: 'Shopping for Men: The Single Woman Narrative'. *Women: A Cultural Review*, 11 (3), 238–51.

Putnam, R. 1995: 'Bowling Alone: America's Declining Social Capital'. *Journal of Democracy*, 6 (1), 71–8.

Roberts, J. 1999: 'Dogme 95', *New Left Review*, 238, November/December, 141–9.

Bibliography

Shields, R. 1990: 'The "System of Pleasure": Liminality and the Carnivalesque at Brighton'. *Theory, Culture and Society*, 7 (1).

Smith, J. 1997: 'Diana: une femme du passé'. *Le Monde Diplomatique*, October, 32.

Wilson, E. 1997: 'The Unbearable Lightness of Diana'. *New Left Review*, 226, November/December, 136–45.

Wilson, E. 1999: 'Bohemian Love'. *Theory, Culture and Society*, 15, 3–4.

Plays

Osborne, J. 1956: *Look Back in Anger*.

Newspapers

Independent on Sunday, 21 November 1999.

Guardian, 22 November 1999.

O. James, *Guardian*, January 2000.

Index

Abelard and Héloïse 8, 76
abortion 72, 84, 87–8, 97
adultery 29, 82–3, 117–18;
    see also infidelity
age difference: marriage 9,
    13; sexual relationships
    25–6
age of consent 12–13
alienation 127–8
Almodavar, Pedro 115
Amis, Martin 118–19
Anglican marriage ceremony
    10, 145n13
Anglo-Saxon cultures 92–3
Archer, Jeffrey 94–5, 98, 117
Archer, Mary 98–9, 117
Arendt, Hannah 122, 128
Aries, Philip 128
aristocracy 10, 82–3
Auden, W. H. 79
Austen, Jane 113;
    Enlightenment morality
    28, 29; erotic 77; love/
    desire 77; Mansfield Park
    31–3, 56; marriage/love

42; men/women 46–7;
    Pride and Prejudice
    29–30, 137; rationality
    34–5, 46–7; romance 32;
    Sanditon 138; Sense and
    Sensibility 31, 34, 70–1,
    138
Austin Powers film 60
authority/paternity 112–13
autonomy 132–3, 134

Barstow, Stan: A Kind of
    Loving 83, 89–90, 96
Basic Instinct film 84
Beauvoir, Simone de 80–1
Beck, Ulrich 3, 53, 54, 124,
    130, 141
Beck-Gernsheim, Elisabeth
    53, 54, 113, 130, 141
behavioural rules 74, 134–5
Bell, Vanessa 61
Benjamin, Walter 108
Bennett, Arnold 44
birth rate 49
blindness of love 79–80

body 16, 63, 86–7
bohemianism 114–15
Bourdieu, Pierre 69
Brontë, Charlotte: erotic 28;
    falling in love 41; *Jane
    Eyre* 28, 29, 35–7, 41,
    91; marriage/love 42;
    romance 36
Brontë, Emily 42; *Wuthering
    Heights* 41–2
Brook Advisory Centre 89
Brown, Judith 8
Burchill, Julie 11
bureaucracy 27, 45, 77, 129
Butler, Judith 17
Byron, Lord 81

Campbell, Beatrix 11
capitalism 42, 127–8
capitalism, late: consumerism
    136; love 23; personhood
    138; sex industry 74;
    time-poor individuals 54;
    victims 141–2
Cartland, Barbara 18
Castle, Terry 27
Caulfield, Mr Justice 98–9
censorship 56–7, 149n6
change/tradition 115
chaos of love 54–5, 130
Chaplin, Charlie 45
Charles, Prince of Wales:
    engagement interview
    8–9; expectations of
    marriage 8–10; family
    10; intimacy 15–16; love
    8–9, 22; normality 15;
    wedding clothes 13–14
chastity 47
chat lines 59
child prostitution 91

children: as consequence of
    love 81; costs of having
    51–2, 111–12; desire for
    96; divorce 20, 102,
    130–2, 153n7; foster
    parents 113–14; love of
    1, 104, 111–12; paternity
    96, 97, 112–13;
    prioritising male 95;
    relationship break-up 6,
    102, 113; separation 20;
    sexual abuse 110;
    sexualization 61–2;
    single-parent family 49,
    89, 130
Clark, Alan 95–6, 117
Clark, Jane 117
class: cross-impersonation
    17; marriage 10, 37–8;
    morality 95–6; sexual
    advertising 58, 146n22;
    sexuality 71–2; *see also*
    aristocracy
Clinton, Bill 61, 92
Clinton, Hillary 117
clubs échangistes 74–5, 90
Coghlan, Monica 94–5, 98
cohabitation 20, 25–6, 127
commercialization: erotic 68;
    love 75; romance 68;
    sexuality 63, 64, 68,
    74–5
commitment 25, 139, 142
community 108
compartmentalization of lives
    121–2
consumerism: democratization
    105; gender differences
    85; Hoggart 48–9;
    integration 49; late
    capitalism 136; literature

consumerism (*continued*)
69; media 54; seduction
108; taste 69–70
Contagious Diseases Act 88
contraception: availability
89–90, 96, 106–7;
morality 7, 83–4, 89–90,
96; prohibition 72;
responsibility 96–7;
sexualization of marriage
78
control 27, 129; *see also*
discipline
corruption of minors 12
Cosmopolitan 139
courtly love 80
Coward, Ros 52, 53
cross-impersonation 17
culture: democratization
116; global 85, 138–9;
politicians 92–3;
revelatory 126–7;
sexualization 91–2, 120;
see also Western culture
cynicism 74

Daily Star 98
dating agencies 63–4,
148–9n3
Day, Doris 47
deceit 7, 11–12, 116–17,
118; *see also* infidelity
democratization:
consumerism 105;
culture 116; intimacy
3–4, 5, 50, 51, 124–5;
love 124–5; sexual
relationships 135–6
Descartes, René 34, 77
desire: for children 96;
familiarity 81; Freud

108–9, 112, 140; love
23, 24, 77, 109–10;
respect 112; romance 72;
women 82, 83
destabilizing effect 2, 5–6,
48, 49–50
Dickinson, Emily 104
discipline 71; *see also* control
disengagement from politics
122
divorce: Amis 118–19;
business opportunities
5–6; children 20, 102,
130–2, 153n7; Europe
101; financial settlement
130–1; probability of 25,
101–2; remarriage 131;
United States of America
39, 101, 130; Western
culture 18
domesticity 45–6, 52–3,
133–4
Donne, John 2
double standard of morality
88–9, 117, 135
Douglas, Mary: *Purity and
Danger* 99
dress, performance 13–14,
16–17
Dylan, Bob 48

Eastern cultures 66
Eastwood, Clint 93–4
economics/morality 149n12
Ehrenreich, Barbara 62
Elias, Norbert 72–3
Eliot, George 29, 42;
Middlemarch 43
Eliot, T. S.: *Little Gidding* 25
emotion 71, 86–7, 93–4
employment 50, 133, 146n23

engagement 8–9, 38
Engels, Friedrich 80, 81
Enlightenment Project 24, 28,
    29, 76, 114–15
erotic: Austen 77; Brontë
    28; commercialization
    68; fantasy 66, 121;
    forbidden 110;
    regulation 23; repression
    121, 128; sexuality 140,
    143; Western culture
    66–7
European attitudes 101
expectations: female body 63;
    gender differences 42,
    44; happiness 107;
    marriage 8–10, 42, 44,
    101, 132–3; norms 19;
    politicians 92–3;
    relationships 102–3;
    sexual relationships
    135–6
exploitation 128

Faderman, Lillian 27
falling in love 7, 40–1, 70,
    105
Faludi, Susan 52
familiarity/desire 81
family 146n1, 153n7;
    besieged 128; breakdown
    3, 123; destabilization
    48, 49–50; employment
    50; as institution 123;
    post-familial 113; right-
    wing politics 119; single-
    parent 49, 89, 130
fantasy 32–3, 66, 75, 121
female body 63
feminism 21, 62, 125–6
Fielding, Helen: *Bridget*

Jones's Diary 68–9,
    136–7; *The Edge of
    Reason* 116
film representations 45, 60–1,
    104, 149n6
financial independence 133
financial settlements 130–1
Flaubert, Gustave 82;
    Madame Bovary 56,
    116–17, 118
Flett, Kathryn 39–40, 41, 69,
    78, 143
foster parents 113–14
Foucault, Michel 33–4, 91,
    134, 141
Fraser, Nancy 85
free love 135
freedom 5, 7–8, 23
Freud, Sigmund: *Civilization
    and its Discontents* 109;
    desire 108–9, 112, 140;
    moral development 86
future world 84–5

Garfinkel, Harold 17
Gaskell, Elizabeth: marriage
    29, 42; *North and South*
    43; *Ruth* 82
gender: cross-impersonation
    17; identity 17;
    independence 36;
    inequalities 4, 21, 52–3,
    125–6; performance 15
gender differences: adultery
    117–18; consumerism
    85; domesticity 46;
    eradication 84–5;
    expectations of marriage
    42, 44; legal status 82;
    marriage 131; moral
    agency 82, 95–6,

gender differences (*continued*)
98–100; moral reasoning
85–6; power 140;
promiscuity 134–5;
romantic love 46–7, 81,
93; rules of love 82;
sexual permissiveness
62–3
Giddens, Anthony:
androgynous society
132–3; confluent love 50,
51; democratization of
love 124; 'Global Care
Chains' 133; intimacy
3–4, 50, 51, 53, 102;
relationships 3–4, 53–4;
secular marriage 120;
sexual relationships
125–6, 135
Gilligan, Carol 85–6, 100;
In a Different Voice
86–7
Gillis, John 153n7
global culture 85, 138–9
God 76, 77, 100, 103
Godwin, William 1
Goffman, Erving 17
Greer, Germaine 62
Gross, Otto 114

Habermas, Jürgen 7
happiness 19–20, 55, 107
Hefner, Hugh 64–5, 65,
66–7, 74, 112
Hello! 39, 106
heterosexuality as norm 26
Hite, Shere 75
Hochschild, Arlie 50, 133,
134
Hoggart, Richard 48–9,
56–7, 71–2

homosexuality: age of consent
12–13; decriminalized
47; Foucault 134; public
acceptability 127; rules
of behaviour 134–5
Hutton, Will 133
Huxley, Aldous: *Point
Counter Point* 84

identity 17–18
The Idiots 60
incest 109, 110
independence 36, 133; *see
also* autonomy
Independent on Sunday 58
individual: autonomy 132–3,
134; behavioural rules
134–5; capitalism 127;
compartmentalization of
lives 121–2; control 129;
fulfilment 127; happiness
107; intimacy 54, 122;
society 53, 108
inequalities: gender 4, 21,
52–3, 125–6; marriage
21; social 139, 141–2
infidelity 130; *see also*
adultery; deceit
information/interpretation
127
integration, social 49
intimacy: democratization
3–4, 5, 50, 51, 124–5;
Giddens 3–4, 50, 51, 53,
102; individual 54, 122;
loneliness 2; physical
15–16; social/personal
122

Jackson, Stevi 7
James, Oliver 139

Index

Jeffreys, Sheila 62, 63
Johnson, Samuel 106
Jones, Monica 121

Keays, Sarah 94–5, 96–7, 97–8, 98
Kennedy, J. F. 126–7
Klein, Naomi 108
Kohlberg, Lawrence 86
Kumar, Krishan 122

labour market 111
Langford, Wendy 4, 124–5
Larkin, Philip 68, 121–2; 'Annus Mirabilis' 73–4
Lasch, Christopher 50, 128
Lawrence, D. H. 44; *Lady Chatterley's Lover* 56
Lawson, Annette 117, 118
Levy, Amy 120
Lewinsky, Monica 61
Lewis, Sinclair: *Babbit* 44–5
Linley, Viscount 106
literature: censorship 56–7; consumerism 69; marriage 29, 42; romance 75; romantic heroines 136–7; sexual explicitness 57, 75; *see also individual authors*
Lodge, David 121
loneliness 2
love 1, 2, 5–6, 8, 78; blindness 79–80; chaos 54–5, 130; commercialization 75; commitment 142; democratization 124–5; desire 23, 24, 77, 109–10; ending of 80, 101, 113; Foucault 141;

marriage 8, 20, 21–2, 42, 47, 55, 80; metaphors 27, 103, 108; modernization 27; morality 105; need for 125, 143; poverty 51; rationality 143; redemption 45; relationships 26; romance 142; Romantics 28; rules of 82; sexual relationships 76, 106–7; sexuality 140–1, 142–3; sexualization 123; visual perception 70; *see also* falling in love
love, types of: confluent 50, 51; conjugal 76–7; courtly 80; free 135; individualized 7–8; parental 1, 104, 111–12; transcendent 42–3; unconditional 104–5; *see also* romantic love
Love Story film 104
Luhmann, Niklas 124
lust 23

Macbeth 80
McDonaldization 65
McIntosh, Mary 73
Macintyre, Alasdair 32
McLintock, Anne 66
Macmillan, Mrs Harold 126–7
magazines 39, 58, 62, 75, 106, 116
male gaze 64
marriage: age difference 9, 13; Anglican ceremony 10, 145n13; arranged 18,

167

marriage (*continued*)
85; class 10, 37–8;
commitment 25;
disappointments 29–30;
end of love 80;
expectations 8–10,
25, 42, 101, 132–3;
feminism 21; financial
settlements 130–1;
gender differences 131;
ideals 94–5; inequalities
21; irrelevance 102; in
literature 29, 42; love 8,
20, 21–2, 42, 47, 55,
80; magazines 116;
masquerade 13–14;
motivation 21;
negotiation 137–8; open
118; patriarchy 9, 98;
pregnancy 47; property
132–3; rites of passage
114; romantic love 29,
43; same sex 116;
secularization 77–8,
120; sexuality 107;
sexualization 77–8, 112;
shot-gun 83, 89; social
contract 10, 76; tradition
14; as trap 44
marriage contracts 132–3
Marx, Karl 127–8
masculinity 15, 44, 52, 93–4
masquerade 13–14, 15
maternity: *see* motherhood
media: consumerism 54;
Diana Spencer 14;
revelation 126–7; sexual
relationships 94–5,
126–7; wealth 105–6;
see also films; magazines
memory 25

men: desire/love 82, 109–10;
emotion 93–4; gaze 64;
moral agenda 98–9;
promiscuity 134–5;
violence 110; *see also*
gender differences;
masculinity
mind/body separation 86–7
Modern Times film 45
modernity, late 53, 81
modernization 7, 27, 100
moral agency 82, 95–6,
98–100
morality 85–6; abortion
87–8; class 95–6;
contraception 7, 83–4,
89–90, 96; double
standard 88–9, 117, 135;
economics 149n12;
Enlightenment Project
28; love 105; new 22;
reasoning 85–6; scientific
knowledge 100–1; sexual
relationships 83–4;
sexuality 12–13, 84, 90
mother–child relationship
132
motherhood 110–11, 132
Mozart, Wolfgang Amadeus:
Così fan tutte 143,
154n18; *The Magic Flute*
52

Nature 24, 103
New Statesman 58
Nietzsche, Friedrich 112
norms 15, 19, 26
Nussbaum, Martha 85

OK 39
organization man 44–5

Orwell, George: *1984* 44–5, 46, 47, 49, 84, 143; *Coming Up for Air* 45; domesticity 45–6; predictions 54
Osborne, John 44
Othello 80

parental love 1, 104, 111–12
Paris and Helen of Troy 80
Parkinson, Ann 95, 98
Parkinson, Cecil 94–5, 96–7, 98
Parnell, Charles 61
Parsons, Talcott 7
Parsons, Tony: *Man and Boy* 112
paternity 96, 97, 112–13
patriarchy 9, 48, 82, 98, 106–7
Penguin Books 56, 57
People 106
performance 13–14, 15, 16–18
perjury 94, 98
permissive society 47, 57, 74, 85
personhood 138
Philips, Deborah 69
Phillips, Melanie 3
physical attraction 34, 136; *see also* sexual attraction
Plath, Sylvia: *The Bell Jar* 43–4
Playboy 62
Playboy clubs 64–5, 112
politicians 61, 92–3, 94–5
politics: disengagement 122; right-wing 97, 119, 149n12
popular music 47–8

pornography 112, 121
postmodern world 53
poverty 51
power 67, 124–5, 126, 140
predation, sexual 99
pregnancy: contraception 89–90; fear of 73; marriage 47, 89, 90–1; responsibility 96–7; transient sexual relationships 83, 84; unwanted 89, 90–1
pre-nuptial contracts 132–3
Profumo, John 61
promiscuity 134–5
property 132–3
prostitution 60, 63–4, 91
public–private distinctions 81–2, 122, 136
Putnam, Robert 122

rationality 34–5, 46–7, 128–30, 143
Rattigan, Terence 93
reality/romance 18
reason/emotion 86–7
relationships: ending 4; expectations 102–3; Giddens 3–4, 53–4; love 26; parents 6, 102, 113; pure 3; sexual liberalization 139–40; single person household 139–40; *see also* sexual relationships
remarriage 106, 119, 131
repression 71, 121, 128
respect/desire 112
responsibility 96–7
Restoration drama 80
revelatory culture 126–7

rites of passage 114, 129
Roman Catholicism 120–1
romance: Austen 32; Brontë
     36; capitalism 42;
     commercialization 68;
     death of 84; desire 72;
     Enlightenment Project
     76; lifelong entitlement
     123; literature 75,
     136–7; love 142; public
     appetite 38, 39; reality
     18; scepticism 21; sexual
     relationships 6–7
romantic love: gender
     differences 46–7, 81,
     93; global culture 85;
     limitations 119; marriage
     43; modernization 7,
     100; valorization 2, 128
Romanticism 28, 71
Romeo and Juliet 8, 76, 80
Roosevelt, T. 126–7
Rose, Gillian 20
rules of behaviour 134–5
rules of love 82

Said, Edward 66
St Valentine's Day 63
same sex marriage 116
same sex relationships 27,
     28–9; *see also*
     homosexuality
Sammy and Rosie Get Laid
     film 60
scepticism 21
science fiction 84
scientific knowledge/morality
     100–1
secularization of marriage
     77–8, 120
seduction 32–3, 108

Sennett, Richard 108
separation 5–6, 18, 20
sex industry 63–4, 74
sex tourism 63, 65–6
sexual abuse 110
sexual attraction 7–8, 37,
     137; *see also* physical
     appearance
sexual explicitness 57, 60–1,
     75
sexual liberalization 62, 63,
     126–7, 139–40
sexual permissiveness 62–3,
     78
sexual relationships 1;
     advertising for 57–60,
     146n22; age difference
     25–6; casual 7, 60,
     83–4; childbearing 111;
     civilized 73; Clinton 61;
     clubs échangistes 74–5;
     democratization 135–6;
     expectations 135–6; free
     love 135; Giddens
     125–6, 135; irrelevance
     of marriage 102; love
     76, 106–7; media 94–5,
     126–7; need for 59;
     old/new morality 83–4;
     personalized 60;
     politicians 61, 92–3,
     94–5; power 126;
     recreational 62;
     renegotiations 50, 51;
     responsibility 97; rites
     of passage 114, 129;
     romantic attachment
     6–7; social change 37,
     115–16
sexuality: class 71–2;
     commercialization 63,

64, 68, 74–5; erotic 140,
143; fantasy 75; Foucault
91; illicit 98–9; love
140–1, 142–3; marriage
107; maternity 110–11;
morality 12–13, 84, 90;
patriarchy 82; popular
music 47–8; power 67,
124–5; premarital 114;
regulation of 33–4, 91;
repression 71, 121;
Roman Catholicism
120–1; rules of
behaviour 134–5;
transgression 83;
Victorian 67, 91;
Western culture 7, 60
sexualization: children 61–2;
culture 91–2, 120; love
123; marriage 77–8,
112
Shelley, Mary: *Frankenstein*
100–1
Shelley, P. B. 28
silencing of women's voice
86
Sillitoe, Alan: *Saturday Night
and Sunday Morning* 83
Simmel, Georg 7, 108, 140
single-parent family 49, 89,
130
single person household 49,
122, 123, 139–40
slavery 7, 108
Smith, Joan 12
Smith-Rosenberg, Carol 27
social contract 10, 76
social exclusion 139
social inequality 139, 141–2
social life: adultery 83;
compartments 121–2;

destabilization 2, 5–6;
fragmentation 3;
intimacy 122; rules 82;
sexual relationships 37,
115–16
society: androgynous 132–3;
change 115–16; control
129; individual 53, 108;
integration 49
sociologists 7
soulmate 41
Soviet Union 85
space/body 16
Spain 115
Spencer, Diana: characteristics
12, 15–16; death 14;
expectations 8–11;
family 10; femininity 15;
identity performance 17,
18; illness 16; marriage
25; media 14; public
mourning for 11;
wedding dress 13–14
Stanley, Liz 27
state socialism 85
Stead, W. T. 91
Steinem, Gloria 65
stigmatization 73, 131
Stone, Lawrence 153n7
Stopes, Marie 107
Strachey, Lytton 61
subjectivity/objectivity 81–2
subversiveness 34–5
succession 10, 11
surveillance 33–4

Tanner, Tony 29, 76
taste 69–70
The Tatler 58
Taylor, A. J. P. 49
Thatcher, Margaret 53

Time Out 58
time poor individuals 54,
    148n38
Titmuss, Richard 49
Tolstoy, Leo: *Anna Karenina*
    2, 23, 82–3, 93, 116–17,
    118, 140; *War and Peace*
    93
Tonnies, Ferdinand 108
tradition 14, 38–9, 115,
    147n15
transgression 80, 83, 114–15

unconditionality of love
    104–5
unconnectedness 108
unemployment 142
United States of America:
    constitution 20;
    disengagement from
    politics 122; divorce 39,
    101, 130; marriage
    contracts 132–3;
    presidents 61, 92, 126–7
unselfishness 79
Updike, John: *Couples* 118

Verhoeven, Paul 84
victims 81, 141–2
Victorian sexuality 67, 91
Vietnam war protestors
    4–5
violence 110
visual perception 70

Vogue 58
voice of women 86, 87, 88

wealth: media 105–6; social
    inequality 139, 141–2
Weber, Max 7, 27, 108, 114,
    127, 128–30
wedding anniversaries 39
weddings 13–14, 38–9, 115
Weeks, Jeffrey 124
Wells, H. G. 44
Western culture: divorce 18;
    erotic 66–7; fascination
    with East 66; freedom
    5; love 1, 2, 8; moral
    discourse 85–6; sexual
    relationships 7, 60
Whitehouse, Mary 90
Wilson, Elizabeth 12, 114
Windsor, Lady Helen 106
Windsor family 10, 19
women: autonomy 133;
    bureaucracy 45; desire
    82, 83; disposability 95;
    emancipation 84–5;
    financial independence
    133; good/bad 98–9;
    silenced 86, 87, 88;
    victims 81; *see also*
    gender differences;
    motherhood
Wordsworth, William:
    'Tintern Abbey' 124
work 50, 133–4, 146n23

Index compiled by Zeb Korycinska